Swimming Chenango Lake: Selected Poems

Charles Tomlinson was born in Stoke on Trent in 1927. He studied at Cambridge with Donald Davie and taught at the University of Bristol from 1956 until his retirement. He published many collections of poetry as well as volumes of criticism and translation, and edited the *Oxford Book of Verse in Translation* (1980). His poetry won international recognition and received many prizes in Europe and the United States, including the 1993 Bennett Award from the Hudson Review; the New Criterion Poetry Prize, 2002; the Premio Internazionale di Poesia Ennio Flaiano, 2001; and the Premio Internazionale di Poesia Attilio Bertolucci, 2004. He was an Honorary Fellow of Queens' College, Cambridge, the American Academy of the Arts and Sciences, and of the Modern Language Association. Charles Tomlinson was made a CBE in 2001 for his contribution to literature. He died in 2015.

The poet **David Morley**, editor of this volume, is an ecologist and naturalist by background. He won the Ted Hughes Award for New Work in Poetry for *The Invisible Gift: Selected Poems* and a Cholmondeley Award for his contribution to poetry. His Carcanet collections include *The Magic of What's There, The Gypsy and the Poet, Enchantment, The Invisible Kings* and *Scientific Papers*. He wrote *The Cambridge Introduction to Creative Writing* and is co-editor with the Australian poet Philip Neilsen of *The Cambridge Companion to Creative Writing*. David Morley studied with Charles Tomlinson at Bristol and currently teaches at the University of Warwick. He is a Fellow of the Royal Society of Literature.

CW00550594

CHARLES TOMLINSON

Swimming Chenango Lake
SELECTED POEMS

edited by David Morley

Carcanet
Classics

First published in Great Britain in 2018 in the Carcanet Classics series by
Carcanet Press Limited
Alliance House, 30 Cross Street,
Manchester, M2 7AQ
www.carcanet.co.uk

A CIP catalogue record for this book is
available from the British Library,
ISBN 978 1 784106 79 9

The publisher acknowledges financial
assistance from Arts Council England.

Typeset in Great Britain by XL Publishing Services, Exmouth, Devon
Printed in Great Britain by SRP Ltd., Exeter, Devon

Dedication

to Brenda Tomlinson

When you wrote to tell of your arrival,
　　It was midnight, you said, and knew
In wishing me *Goodnight* that I
　　Would have been long abed. And that was true.
I was dreaming your way for you, my dear,
　　Freed of the mist that followed the snow here,
And yet it followed you (within my dream, at least)
　　Nor could I close my dreaming eye
To the thought of further snow
　　Widening the landscape as it sought
The planes and ledges of your moorland drive.
　　I saw a scene climb up around you
That whiteness had marked out and multiplied
　　With a thousand touches beyond the green
And calculable expectations summer in such a place
　　Might breed in one. My eye took in
Close-to, among the vastnesses you passed unharmed,
　　The shapes the frozen haze hung on the furze
Like scattered necklaces the frost had caught
　　Half-unthreaded in their fall. It must have been
The firm prints of your midnight pen
　　Over my fantasia of snow, told you were safe,
Turning the threats from near and far
　　To images of beauty we might share
As we shared my dream that now
　　Flowed to the guiding motion of your hand,
As though through the silence of propitious dark
　　It had reached out to touch me across sleeping England.

from 'Winter Journey', *The Return* (1987)

Acknowledgements

The editor thanks Anne Ashworth, Ian Brinton, John Greening, Peter Larkin, Michael Schmidt, Justine and Juliet Tomlinson, and William Wootton for their contributions to the realisation of this book. The largest debt of gratitude is to Brenda Tomlinson, without whom it would not exist.

Contents

A Peopled Landscape (1963)

American Scenes and Other Poems (1966)

The Way of a World (1969)

The Flood (1981)

Notes from New York and Other Poems (1984)

The Return (1987)

Annunciations (1989)

The Door in the Wall (1992)

Jubilation (1995)

The Vineyard above the Sea (1999)

Skywriting (2003)

Cracks in the Universe (2006)

Selected Poems

Prologue

Swimming Chenango Lake

Winter will bar the swimmer soon.
　He reads the water's autumnal hesitations
A wealth of ways: it is jarred,
　It is astir already despite its steadiness,
Where the first leaves at the first
　Tremor of the morning air have dropped
Anticipating him, launching their imprints
　Outwards in eccentric, overlapping circles.
There is a geometry of water, for this
　Squares off the clouds' redundances
And sets them floating in a nether atmosphere
　All angles and elongations: every tree
Appears a cypress as it stretches there
　And every bush that shows the season,
A shaft of fire. It is a geometry and not
　A fantasia of distorting forms, but each
Liquid variation answerable to the theme
　It makes away from, plays before:
It is a consistency, the grain of the pulsating flow.
　But he has looked long enough, and now
Body must recall the eye to its dependence
　As he scissors the waterscape apart
And sways it to tatters. Its coldness
　Holding him to itself, he grants the grasp,
For to swim is also to take hold
　On water's meaning, to move in its embrace
And to be, between grasp and grasping, free.
　He reaches in-and-through to that space
The body is heir to, making a where
　In water, a possession to be relinquished
Willingly at each stroke. The image he has torn

Flows-to behind him, healing itself,
Lifting and lengthening, splayed like the feathers
   Down an immense wing whose darkening spread
Shadows his solitariness: alone, he is unnamed
   By this baptism, where only Chenango bears a name
In a lost language he begins to construe –
   A speech of densities and derisions, of half-
Replies to the questions his body must frame
   Frogwise across the all but penetrable element.
Human, he fronts it and, human, he draws back
   From the interior cold, the mercilessness
That yet shows a kind of mercy sustaining him.
   The last sun of the year is drying his skin
Above a surface a mere mosaic of tiny shatterings,
   Where a wind is unscaping all images in the flowing obsidian
The going-elsewhere of ripples incessantly shaping.

from *The Way of a World* (1969)

Poem

Wakening with the window over fields
To the coin-clear harness-jingle as a float
Clips by, and each succeeding hoof fall, now remote,
Breaks clean and frost-sharp on the unstopped ear.

The hooves describe an arabesque on space,
A dotted line in sound that falls and rises
As the cart goes by, recedes, turns to retrace
Its way back through the unawakened village.

And space vibrates, enlarges with the sound;
Though space is soundless, yet creates
From very soundlessness a ground
To counterstress the lilting hoof fall as it breaks.

Aesthetic

Reality is to be sought, not in concrete,
But in space made articulate:
The shore, for instance,
Spreading between wall and wall;
The sea-voice
Tearing the silence from the silence.

Nine Variations in a Chinese Winter Setting

I
Warm flute on the cold snow
Lays amber in sound.

II
Against brushed cymbal
Grounds yellow on green,
Amber on tinkling ice.

III
The sage beneath the waterfall
Numbers the blessing of a flute;
Water lets down
Exploding silk.

IV
The hiss of raffia,
The thin string scraped with the back of the bow
Are not more bat-like
Than the gusty bamboos
Against a flute.

V

Pine-scent
In snow-clearness
Is not more exactly counterpointed
Than the creak of trodden snow
Against a flute.

VI

The outline of the water-dragon
Is not embroidered with so intricate a thread
As that with which the flute
Defines the tangible borders of a mood.

VII

The flute in summer makes streams of ice:
In winter it grows hospitable.

VIII

In mist, also, a flute is cold
Beside a flute in snow.

IX

Degrees of comparison
Go with differing conditions:
Sunlight mellows lichens,
Whereas snow mellows the flute.

Sea Change

To define the sea –
We change our opinions
With the changing light.

Light struggles with colour:
A quincunx
Of five stones, a white
Opal threatened by emeralds.

The sea is uneasy marble.

The sea is green silk.

The sea is blue mud, churned
By the insistence of wind.

Beneath dawn a sardonyx may be cut from it
In white layers laced with a carnelian orange,
A leek- or apple-green chalcedony
Hewn in the cold light.

Illustration is white wine
Floating in a saucer of ground glass
On a pedestal of cut glass:

A static instance, therefore untrue.

The Art of Poetry

At first, the mind feels bruised.
The light makes white holes through the black foliage
Or mist hides everything that is not itself.

But how shall one say so? –
The fact being, that when the truth is not good enough
We exaggerate. Proportions

Matter. It is difficult to get them right.
There must be nothing
Superfluous, nothing which is not elegant
And nothing which is if it is merely that.

This green twilight has violet borders.

Yellow butterflies
Nervously transferring themselves
From scarlet to bronze flowers
Disappear as the evening appears.

Fiascherino

Over an ash-fawn beach fronting a sea which keeps
    Rolling and unrolling, lifting
The green fringes from submerged rocks
    On its way in, and, on its way out
Dropping them again, the light

Squanders itself, a saffron morning
    Advances among foam and stones, sticks
Clotted with black naphtha
    And frayed to the newly carved
Fresh white of chicken flesh.

One leans from the cliff-top. Height
    Distances like an inverted glass; the shore
Is diminished but concentrated, jewelled
    With the clarity of warm colours
That, seen more nearly, would dissipate

Into masses. The map-like interplay
    Of sea-light against shadow
And the mottled close-up of wet rocks
    Drying themselves in the hot air
Are lost to us. Content with our portion,

Where, we ask ourselves, is the end of all this
    Variety that follows us? Glare
Pierces muslin; its broken rays
    Hovering in trembling filaments
Glance on the ceiling with no more substance

Than a bee's wing. Thickening, these
    Hang down over the pink walls
In green bars, and, flickering between them,
    A moving fan of two colours,
The sea unrolls and rolls itself into the low room.

The Atlantic

Launched into an opposing wind, hangs
   Grappled beneath the onrush,
And there, lifts, curling in spume,
   Unlocks, drops from that hold
Over and shoreward. The beach receives it,
   A whitening line, collapsing
Powdering-off down its broken length;
   Then, curded, shallow, heavy
With clustering bubbles, it nears
   In a slow sheet that must climb
Relinquishing its power, upward
   Across tilted sand. Unravelled now
And the shore, under its lucid pane,
   Clear to the sight, it is spent:
The sun rocks there, as the netted ripple
   Into whose skeins the motion threads it
Glances athwart a bed, honeycombed
   By heaving stones. Neither survives the instant
But is caught back, and leaves, like the after-image
   Released from the floor of a now different mind,
A quick gold, dyeing the uncovering beach
   With sunglaze. That which we were,
Confronted by all that we are not,
   Grasps in subservience its replenishment.

Oxen: Ploughing at Fiesole

The heads, impenetrable
And the slow bulk
Soundless and stooping,
A white darkness – burdened
Only by sun, and not
By the matchwood yoke –
They groove in ease
The meadow through which they pace
Tractable. It is as if
Fresh from the escape,
They consent to submission,
The debris of captivity
Still clinging there
Unnoticed behind those backs:
'But we submit' – the tenor
Unambiguous in that stride
Of even confidence –
'Giving and not conceding
Your premises. Work
Is necessary, therefore –'
(With an unsevered motion
Holding the pauses
Between stride and stride)
'We will be useful
But we will not be swift: now
Follow us for your improvement
And at our pace.' This calm
Bred from this strength, and the reality
Broaching no such discussion,
The man will follow, each
As the other's servant
Content to remain content.

How Still the Hawk

How still the hawk
Hangs innocent above
Its native wood:
Distance, that purifies the act
Of all intent, has graced
Intent with beauty.
Beauty must lie
As innocence must harm
Whose end (sited,
Held) is naked
Like the map it cowers on.
And the doom drops:
Plummet of peace
To him who does not share
The nearness and the need,
The shrivelled circle
Of magnetic fear.

Glass Grain

The glare goes down. The metal of a molten pane
Cast on the wall with red light burning through,
Holds in its firm, disordered square, the shifting strands
The glass conceals, till (splitting sun) it dances
Lanterns in lanes of light its own streaked image.
Like combed-down hair. Like weathered wood, where
Line, running with, crowds on line and swaying
Rounding each knot, yet still keeps keen
The perfect parallel. Like... in likes, what do we look for?
Distinctions? That, but not that in sum. Think of the fugue's
    theme:
After inversions and divisions, doors
That no keys can open, cornered conceits
Apprehensions, all ways of knowledge past,
Eden comes round again, the motive dips
Back to its shapely self, its naked nature
Clothed by comparison alone – related. We ask
No less, watching suggestions that a beam selects
From wood, from water, from a muslin-weave,
Swerving across our window, on our wall
(Transparency teased out) the grain of glass.

Tramontana at Lerici

Today, should you let fall a glass it would
    Disintegrate, played off with such keenness
Against the cold's resonance (the sounds
    Hard, separate and distinct, dropping away
In a diminishing cadence) that you might swear
    This was the imitation of glass falling.

Leaf-dapples sharpen. Emboldened by this clarity
    The minds of artificers would turn prismatic,
Running on lace perforated in crisp wafers
    That could cut like steel. Constitutions,
Drafted under this fecund chill, would be annulled
    For the strictness of their equity, the moderation of their pity.

At evening, one is alarmed by such definition
    In as many lost greens as one will give glances to recover,
As many again which the landscape
    Absorbing into the steady dusk, condenses
From aquamarine to that slow indigo-pitch
    Where the light and twilight abandon themselves.

And the chill grows. In this air
    Unfit for politicians and romantics
Dark hardens from blue, effacing the windows:
    A tangible block, it will be no accessory
To that which does not concern it. One is ignored
    By so much cold suspended in so much night.

Paring the Apple

There are portraits and still-lifes.

And there is paring the apple.

And then? Paring it slowly,
From under cool-yellow
Cold-white emerging. And ...?

The spring of concentric peel
Unwinding off white,
The blade hidden, dividing.

There are portraits and still-lifes
And the first, because 'human'
Does not excel the second, and
Neither is less weighted
With a human gesture, than paring the apple
With a human stillness.

The cool blade
Severs between coolness, apple-rind
Compelling a recognition.

More Foreign Cities

Nobody wants any more poems about foreign cities...
          (From a recent disquisition on poetics)

Not forgetting Ko-jen, that
Musical city (it has
Few buildings and annexes
Space by combating silence),
There is Fiordiligi, its sun-changes
Against walls of transparent stone
Unsettling all preconception – a city
For architects (they are taught
By casting their nets
Into those moving shoals); and there is
Kairouan, whose lit space
So slides into and fits
The stone masses, one would doubt
Which was the more solid
Unless, folding back
Gold segments out of the white
Pith globe of a quartered orange,
One may learn perhaps
To read such perspectives. At Luna
There is a city of bridges, where
Even the inhabitants are mindful
Of a shared privilege: a bridge
Does not exist for its own sake.
It commands vacancy.

A Meditation on John Constable

Painting is a science, and should be pursued as an inquiry into the laws of nature.
Why, then, may not landscape painting be considered as a branch of natural
philosophy, of which pictures are but the experiments?
                                    John Constable, *The History of Landscape Painting*

He replied to his own question, and with the unmannered
   Exactness of art; enriched his premises
By confirming his practice: the labour of observation
   In face of meteorological fact. Clouds
Followed by others, temper the sun in passing
   Over and off it. Massed darks
Blotting it back, scattered and mellowed shafts
   Break damply out of them, until the source
Unmasks, floods its retreating bank
   With raw fire. One perceives (though scarcely)
The remnant clouds trailing across it
   In rags, and thinned to a gauze.
But the next will dam it. They loom past
   And narrow its blaze. It shrinks to a crescent
Crushed out, a still lengthening ooze
   As the mass thickens, though cannot exclude
Its silvered-yellow. The eclipse is sudden,
   Seen first on the darkening grass, then complete
In a covered sky.
               Facts. And what are they?
He admired accidents, because governed by laws,
   Representing them (since the illusion was not his end)
As governed by feeling. The end is our approval
   Freely accorded, the illusion persuading us
That it exists as a human image. Caught
   By a wavering sun, or under a wind
Which moistening among the outlines of banked foliage
   Prepares to dissolve them, it must grow constant;
Though there, ruffling and parted, the disturbed
   Trees let through the distance, like white fog
Into their broken ranks. It must persuade
   And with a constancy, not to be swept back
To reveal what it half-conceals. Art is itself

Once we accept it. The day veers. He would have judged
Exactly in such a light, that strides down
   Over the quick stains of cloud-shadows
Expunged now, by its conflagration of colour.
   A descriptive painter? If delight
Describes, which wrings from the brush
   The errors of a mind, so tempered,
It can forgo all pathos; for what he saw
   Discovered what he was, and the hand – unswayed
By the dictation of a single sense –
   Bodied the accurate and total knowledge
In a calligraphy of present pleasure. Art
   Is complete when it is human. It is human
Once the looped pigments, the pin-heads of light
   Securing space under their deft restrictions
Convince, as the index of a possible passion,
   As the adequate gauge, both of the passion
And its object. The artist lies
   For the improvement of truth. Believe him.

Farewell to Van Gogh

The quiet deepens. You will not persuade
    One leaf of the accomplished, steady, darkening
Chestnut-tower to displace itself
    With more of violence than the air supplies
When, gathering dusk, the pond brims evenly
    And we must be content with stillness.

Unhastening, daylight withdraws from us its shapes
    Into their central calm. Stone by stone
Your rhetoric is dispersed until the earth
    Becomes once more the earth, the leaves
A sharp partition against cooling blue.

Farewell, and for your instructive frenzy
    Gratitude. The world does not end tonight
And the fruit that we shall pick tomorrow
    Await us, weighing the unstripped bough.

Cézanne at Aix

And the mountain: each day
Immobile like fruit. Unlike, also
– Because irreducible, because
Neither a component of the delicious
And therefore questionable,
Nor distracted (as the sitter)
By his own pose and, therefore,
Doubly to be questioned: it is not
Posed. It is. Untaught
Unalterable, a stone bridgehead
To that which is tangible
Because unfelt before. There
In its weathered weight
Its silence silences, a presence
Which does not present itself.

At Holwell Farm

It is a quality of air, a temperate sharpness
    Causes an autumn fire to burn compact,
To cast from a shapely and unrifted core
    Its steady brightness. A kindred flame
Gathers within the stone, and such a season
    Fosters, then frees it in a single glow:
Pears by the wall and stone as ripe as pears
    Under the shell-hood's cornice; the door's
Bright oak, the windows' slim-cut frames
    Are of an equal whiteness. Crude stone
By a canopy of shell, each complements
    In opposition, each is bound
Into a pattern of utilities – this farm
    Also a house, this house a dwelling.
Rooted in more than earth, to dwell
    Is to discern the Eden image, to grasp
In a given place and guard it well
    Shielded in stone. Whether piety
Be natural, is neither the poet's
    Nor the builder's story, but a quality of air,
Such as surrounds and shapes an autumn fire
    Bringing these sharp disparities to bear.

Civilities of Lamplight

Without excess (no galaxies
Gauds, illiterate exclamations)
It betokens haven,
An ordering, the darkness held
But not dismissed. One man
Alone with his single light
Wading obscurity refines the instance,
Hollows the hedge-bound track, a sealed
Furrow on dark, closing behind him.

Fire in a Dark Landscape

And where it falls, a quality
Not of the night, but of the mind
As when, on the moonlit roofs,
A counterfeit snow
Whitely deceives us. And yet...
It is the meeting, of light
With dark, challenges the memory
To reveal itself, in an unfamiliar form,
As here: red branches
Into a transparency
In liquid motion, the winds'
Chimera of silk, twisting
Thickened with amber shadows,
A quality, not of the mind
But of fire on darkness.

Winter-Piece

You wake, all windows blind – embattled sprays
grained on the medieval glass.
Gates snap like gunshot
as you handle them. Five-barred fragility
sets flying fifteen rooks who go together
silently ravenous above this winter-piece
that will not feed them. They alight
beyond, scavenging, missing everything
but the bladed atmosphere, the white resistance.
Ruts with iron flanges track
through a hard decay
where you discern once more
oak-leaf by hawthorn, for the frost
rewhets their edges. In a perfect web
blanched along each spoke
and circle of its woven wheel,
the spider hangs, grasp unbroken
and death-masked in cold. Returning
you see the house glint-out behind
its holed and ragged glaze,
frost-fronds all streaming.

The Farmer's Wife: At Fostons Ash

Scent
          from the apple-loft!
                    I smelt it and I saw
in thought
          behind the oak
                    that cupboards all your wine
the store in maturation
          webbed
                    and waiting.
There
          we paused in talk,
                    the labyrinth of lofts
above us and the stair
          beneath, bound
                    for a labyrinth of cellars.
Everywhere
          as darkness
                    leaned and loomed
the light was crossing it
          or travelled through
                    the doors you opened
into rooms that view
          your hens and herds,
                    your cider-orchard.
Proud
          you were
                    displaying these
inheritances
          to an eye
                    as pleased as yours
and as familiar almost
          with them. Mine
                    had known,
had grown into the ways
          that regulate such riches
                    and had seen
your husband's mother's day
          and you had done

     no violence to that recollection,
proving it
  by present fact.
     Distrust
that poet who must symbolize
    your stair into
      an analogue
of what was never there.
     Fact
      has its proper plenitude
that only time and tact
    will show, renew.
     It is enough
those steps should be
    no more than what they were, that your
      hospitable table
overlook the cowshed.
    A just geography
      completes itself
with such relations, where
    beauty and stability can be
      each other's equal.
But building is
    a biding also
      and I saw
one lack
    among your store of blessings.
     You had come
late into marriage
    and your childlessness
      was palpable
as we surveyed
    the kitchen, where four unheraldic
      sheep-dogs kept the floor
and seemed to want
    their complement of children.
     Not desolateness
changed the scene I left,
    the house
      manning its hill,

the gabled bulk
    still riding there
            as though it could
command the crops
    upwards
            out of willing land;
and yet
    it was as if
        a doubt
within my mood
        troubled the rock of its ancestral certitude.

The Hand at Callow Hill Farm

Silence. The man defined
The quality, ate at his separate table
Silent, not because silence was enjoined
But was his nature. It shut him round
Even at outdoor tasks, his speech
Following upon a pause, as though
A hesitance to comply had checked it –
Yet comply he did, and willingly:
Pause and silence: both
Were essential graces, a reticence
Of the blood, whose calm concealed
The tutelary of that upland field.

The Picture of J. T. in a Prospect of Stone

What should one
             wish a child
                          and that, one's own
emerging
             from between
                          the stone lips
of a sheep-stile
             that divides
                          village graves
and village green?
             – Wish her
                          the constancy of stone.
– But stone
             is hard.
                          – Say, rather
it resists
             the slow corrosives
                          and the flight
of time
             and yet it takes
                          the play, the fluency
from light.
             – How would you know
                          the gift you'd give
was the gift
             she'd wish to have?
                          – Gift is giving,
gift is meaning:
             first
                          I'd give
then let her
             live with it
                          to prove
its quality the better and
             thus learn
                          to love
what (to begin with)
             she might spurn.

                        – You'd
moralize a gift?
                  – I'd have her
                          understand
the gift I gave her.
                  – And so she shall
                          but let her play
her innocence away
                  emerging
                          as she does
between
          her doom (unknown),
                    her unmown green.

Up at La Serra

The shadow
  ran before it lengthening
    and a wave went over.
Distance
  did not obscure
    the machine of nature:
you could watch it
  squander and recompose itself
    all day, the shadow-run
the sway of the necessity down there
  at the cliff-base
    crushing white from blue.
Come in
  by the arch
    under the campanile parrocchiale
and the exasperation of the water
  followed you,
    its *Soldi, soldi*
unpicking the hill-top peace
  insistently.
      He knew, at twenty
all the deprivations such a place
  stored for the man
    who had no more to offer
than a sheaf of verse
  in the style of Quasimodo.
      Came the moment,
he would tell it
  in a poem
    without rancour, a lucid
testament above his name
  Paolo
    Bertolani
– *Ciao, Paolo!*
  – *Ciao*
    Giorgino!
He would put them
  all in it –

Giorgino going
over the hill
to look for labour;
the grinder
of knives and scissors
waiting to come up, until
someone would hoist his wheel
on to a back, already
hooped to take it,
so you thought
the weight must crack
the curvature. And then:
Beppino and Beppino
friends
who had in common
nothing except their names and friendship;
and the sister of the one
who played the accordion
and under all
the *Soldi, soldi,*
sacra conversazione
del mare –
della madre.
Sometimes
the men had an air of stupefaction:
La Madre:
it was the women there
won in a truceless enmity.
At home
a sepia-green
Madonna di Foligno
shared the wall
with the October calendar –
Lenin looked out of it,
Mao
blessing the tractors
and you told
the visitors:
We are not communists
although we call ourselves communists

we are what you English
    would call… socialists.
        He believed
that God was a hypothesis,
    that the party would bring in
        a synthesis, that he
would edit the local paper for them,
    or perhaps
        go northward to Milan;
or would he grow
    as the others had – son
        to the puttana-madonna
in the curse,
    chafed by the maternal knot and by
        the dream of faithlessness,
uncalloused hands,
    lace, white
        at the windows of the sailors' brothels
in the port five miles away?
    Soldi –
        soldi –
some
    worked at the naval yards
        and some, like him
were left between
    the time the olives turned
        from green to black
and the harvest of the grapes,
    idle
        except for hacking wood.
Those
    with an acre of good land
        had vines, had wine
and self-respect. Some
    carried down crickets
        to the garden of the mad Englishwoman
who could
    not
        tolerate
crickets, and they received

soldi, soldi
　　for recapturing them...
The construction
　　continued as heretofore
　　　　on the villa of the Milanese dentist
as the evening
　　came in with news:
　　　　– *We have won*
the election.
　　　– At the café
　　　　the red flag is up.
He turned back
　　quickly beneath the tower.
　　　　Giorgino
who wanted to be a waiter
　　wanted to be commissar
　　　　piling *sassi*
into the dentist's wall.
　　Even the harlot's mother
　　　　who had not dared
come forth because her daughter
　　had erred in giving birth,
　　　　appeared by the *Trattoria della Pace.*
She did not enter
　　the masculine precinct,
　　　　listening there, her shadow
lengthened-out behind her
　　black as the uniform of age
　　　　she wore
on back and head.
　　This was the Day
　　　　which began all reckonings
she heard them say
　　with a woman's ears;
　　　　she liked
the music from the wireless.
　　The padre
　　　　pulled
at his unheeded angelus
　　and the Day went down behind

            the town in the bay below
where – come the season –
        they would be preparing
            with striped umbrellas,
for the *stranieri* and *milanesi* –
        treason so readily compounded
            by the promiscuous stir
on the iridescent sliding water.
        He had sought
            the clear air of the cliff.
– *Salve, Giorgino*
        – *Salve*
            Paolo, have you
heard
        that we have won the election?
            – *I am writing*
a poem about it:
        it will begin
            here, with the cliff and with the sea
following its morning shadow in.

Head Hewn with an Axe

The whittled crystal: fissured
For the invasion of shadows.

The stone book, its
Hacked leaves
Frozen in granite.

The meteorite, anatomized
By the geometer. And to what end?
To the enrichment of the alignment:
Sun against shade against sun:
That daily food, which
Were it not for such importunities
Would go untasted:

The suave block, desecrated
In six strokes. The light
Is staunching its wounds.

The Snow Fences

They are fencing the upland against
the drifts this wind, those clouds
would bury it under: brow and bone
know already that levelling zero
as you go, an aching skeleton,
in the breathtaking rareness of winter air.

Walking here, what do you see?
Little more, through wind-teased eyes,
than a black, iron tree
and, there, another, a straggle
of low and broken wall between, grass
sapped of its greenness, day going.

The farms are few: spread
as wide, perhaps, as when
the Saxons who found them, chose
these airy and woodless spaces
and froze here before they fed
the unsuperseded burial ground.

Ahead, the church's dead-white
limewash will dazzle the mind
as, dazed, you enter to escape:
despite the stillness here, the chill
of wash-light scarcely seems
less penetrant than the hill-top wind.

Between the graves, you find
a beheaded pigeon, the blood and grain
trailed from its bitten crop, as alien to all
the day's pallor as the raw
wounds of the earth, turned above
a fresh solitary burial.

A plaque of staining metal
distinguishes this grave among
an anonymity whose stones
the frosts have scaled, thrusting under
as if they grudged the ground
its ill-kept memorials.

The bitter darkness drives you
back valleywards, and again you bend
joint and tendon to encounter
the wind's force and leave behind
the nameless stones, the snow-shrouds
of a waste season: they are fencing
the upland against those years, those clouds.

A Given Grace

Two cups,
a given grace,
afloat and white
on the mahogany pool
of table. They unclench
the mind, filling it
with themselves.
Though common ware,
these rare reflections,
coolness of brown
so strengthens and refines
the burning of their white,
you would not wish
them other than they are –
you, who are challenged
and replenished by
those empty vessels.

Arizona Desert

Eye
drinks the dry orange ground,
the cowskull
bound to it by shade:
sun-warped, the layers
of flaked and broken bone
unclench into petals,
into eyelids of limestone:

Blind glitter
that sees
spaces and steppes expand
of the purgatories possible
to us and
impossible.

Upended trees
in the Hopi's desert orchard
betoken
unceasing unspoken war,
return
the levelling light,
imageless arbiter.

A dead snake
pulsates again
as, hidden, the beetles' hunger
mines through the tunnel of its drying skin.

Here, to be,
is to sound
patience deviously
and follow
like the irregular corn
the water underground.

Villages
from mud and stone
parch back
to the dust they humanize
and mean
marriage, a loving lease
on sand, sun, rock and
Hopi
means peace.

Arroyo Seco

A piano, so long untuned
it sounded like a guitar
was playing *Für Elise*:
the church was locked: graves
on which the only flowers
were the wild ones
except for the everlasting
plastic wreaths and roses,
the bleached dust making
them gaudier than they were
and they were gaudy:

    SILVIANO
    we loved him

    LUCERO

and equal eloquence in
the quotation, twisted and
cut across two pages
in the statuary book:

    THY | LIFE
    WILL | BE
    DO | NE

Ute Mountain

'When I am gone,'
the old chief said
'if you need me, call me,'
and down he lay, became stone.

They were giants then
(as you may see),
and we
are not the shadows of such men.

The long splayed Indian hair
spread ravelling out
behind the rocky head
in groins, ravines;

petered across the desert plain
through Colorado,
transmitting force
in a single undulant unbroken line

from toe to hair-tip: there
profiled, inclined away from one
are features, foreshortened, and the high
blade of the cheekbone.

Reading it so, the eye
can take the entire great
straddle of mountain-mass,
passing down elbows, knees and feet.

'If you need me, call me.'
His singularity dominates the plain
as we call to our aid his image:
thus men make a mountain.

Maine Winter

Ravenous the flock
who with an artist's
tact, dispose
their crow-blue-black
over the spread of snow –
Trackless, save where
by stalled degrees
a fox flaringly goes
with more of the hunter's caution than
of the hunter's ease.

The flock
have sighted him, are his match
and more, with their artist's eye
and a score of beaks against
a fox, paws clogged, and a single pair of jaws.

And they mass to the red-on-white
conclusion, sweep
down between
a foreground all snow-scene and a distance
all cliff-tearing seascape.

The Well

in a Mexican convent

Leaning on
the parapet stone
Listening down
the long, dark
sheath through which the standing
shaft of water
sends its echoings up

Catching, as it stirs
the steady seethings
that mount and mingle
with surrounding sounds
from the neighbouring
barrack-yard: soldiery
– heirs, no doubt
of the gunnery that gashed
these walls of tattered
frescoes, the bullet-
holes now socketed
deeper by sunlight
and the bright gaps
giving on to the square
and there revealing
strollers in khaki
with their girls Aware
of a well-like
cool throughout
the entire, clear
sunlit ruin,
of the brilliant cupids
above the cistern
that hold up
a baldachin of stone
which is not there
Hearing the tide
of insurrection
subside through time
under the still-
painted slogans
Hemos servido
lealmente
la revolución

On a Mexican Straw Christ

This is not the event. This
Is a man of straw,
The legs straw-thin
The straw-arms shent
And nailed. And yet this dry
Essence of agony must be
Close-grained to the one
They lifted down, when
Consummatum est the event was done.
Below the baroque straw-
Haloed basket-head
And the crown, far more
Like a cap, woven
For a matador than a crown of thorn,
A gap recedes: it makes
A mouth-in-pain, the teeth
Within its sideways-slashed
And gritted grin, are
Verticals of straw, and they
Emerge where the mask's
Chin ceases and become
Parallels plunging down, their sum
The body of God. Beneath,
Two feet join in one
Cramped culmination, as if
To say: 'I am the un-
Resurrection and the Death.'

The Oaxaca Bus

Fiat Voluntas Tua:
over the head of the driver
an altar. No end to it,
the beginning seems to be
Our Lady of Solitude
blessing the crowd
out of a double frame –
gilt and green. Dark
mother by light,
her neighbour, the Guadalupe Virgin
is tucked away under the right-
hand edge as if
to make sure
twice over and (left)
are the legs of a protruding
postcard crucifixion
mothered by both. A cosmos
proliferates outwards
from the mystery, starts
with the minute, twin
sombreros dangling there, each
with embroidered brims
and a blood-red cord
circling the crown of each.
The driving mirror
catches their reflection, carries on
the miraculous composition
with two names – serifs
and flourishes –: *Maria,*
Eugenia: both
inscribed on the glass and
flanked at either end
by rampant rockets
torpedoing moonwards. Again
on either side,
an artificial vine
twines down: it is tied
to rails in the aisle

and, along it, flower –
are they nasturtiums? They are
pink like the bathing dresses
of the cut-out belles
it passes in descending,
their petals are pleated
like the green
of the fringed curtain that borders the windshield:
they are lilies
of the field of Mexico,
plastic godsend,
last flourish
of that first Fiat from sister goddesses
and (yes)
the end...

Weeper in Jalisco

A circle of saints, all
hacked, mauled, bound,
bleed in a wooden frieze
under the gloom of the central
dome of gold. They
are in paradise now
and we are not –
baroque feet gone
funnelling up, a blood-
bought, early resurrection
leaving us this
tableau of wounds, the crack
in the universe sealed
behind their flying backs.
We are here, and a woman
sprawls and wails to them
there, the gold screen
glistening, hemming her
under, till her keening
fills the stone ear
of the whole, hollow sanctum
and she is the voice
those wounds cry through
unappeasably bleeding where
her prone back shoulders
the price and weight
of forfeited paradise.

Small Action Poem

for Robert and Bobbie Creeley

To arrive
    unexpectedly
        from nowhere:
then:
    having done
        what it was
one came for,
    to depart.
        The door
is open now
    that before
        was neither
open
    nor was it there.
        It is like
Chopin
    shaking
        music from the fingers,
making that
    in which
        all is either
technique
    heightened to sorcery
        or nothing but notes.
To arrive
    unexpectedly
        at somewhere
and the final
    chord, the final
        word.

Prometheus

Summer thunder darkens, and its climbing
  Cumuli, disowning our scale in the zenith,
Electrify this music: the evening is falling apart.
  Castles-in-air; on earth: green, livid fire.
The radio simmers with static to the strains
  Of this mock last-day of nature and of art.

We have lived through apocalypse too long:
  Scriabin's dinosaurs! Trombones for the transformation
That arrived by train at the Finland Station,
  To bury its hatchet after thirty years in the brain
Of Trotsky. Alexander Nikolayevitch, the events
  Were less merciful than your mob of instruments.

Too many drowning voices cram this waveband.
  I set Lenin's face by yours –
Yours, the fanatic ego of eccentricity against
  The systematic son of a schools inspector
Tyutchev on desk – for the strong man reads
  Poets as the antisemite pleads: 'A Jew was my friend.'

Cymballed firesweeps. Prometheus came down
  In more than orchestral flame and Kerensky fled
Before it. The babel of continents gnaws now
  And tears at the silk of those harmonies that seemed
So dangerous once. You dreamed an end
  Where the rose of the world would go out like a close in music.

Population drags the partitions down
  And we are a single town of warring suburbs:
I cannot hear such music for its consequence:
  Each sense was to have been reborn
Out of a storm of perfumes and light
  To a white world, an in-the-beginning.

In the beginning, the strong man reigns:
    Trotsky, was it not then you brought yourself
To judgement and to execution, when you forgot
    Where terror rules, justice turns arbitrary?
Chromatic Prometheus, myth of fire,
    It is history topples you in the zenith.

Blok, too, wrote The Scythians
    Who should have known: he who howls
With the whirlwind, with the whirlwind goes down.
    In this, was Lenin guiltier than you
When, out of a merciless patience grew
    The daily prose such poetry prepares for?

Scriabin, Blok, men of extremes,
    History treads out the music of your dreams
Through blood, and cannot close like this
    In the perfection of anabasis. It stops. The trees
Continue raining though the rain has ceased
    In a cooled world of incessant codas:

Hard edges of the houses press
    On the after-music senses, and refuse to burn,
Where an ice cream van circulates the estate
    Playing Greensleeves, and at the city's
Stale new frontier even ugliness
    Rules with the cruel mercy of solidities.

*'Prometheus' refers to the tone-poem by Scriabin and to his
hope of transforming the world by music and rite.*

Eden

I have seen Eden. It is a light of place
  As much as the place itself; not a face
Only, but the expression on that face: the gift
  Of forms constellates cliff and stones:
The wind is hurrying the clouds past,
  And the clouds as they flee, ravelling-out
Shadow a salute where the thorn's barb
  Catches the tossed, unroving sack
That echoes their flight. And the same
  Wind stirs in the thicket of the lines
In Eden's wood, the radial avenues
  Of light there, copious enough
To draft a city from. Eden
  Is given one, and the clairvoyant gift
Withdrawn, 'Tell us', we say
  'The way to Eden,' but lost in the meagre
Streets of our dispossession, where
  Shall we turn, when shall we put down
This insurrection of sorry roofs? Despair
  Of Eden is given, too: we earn
Neither its loss nor having. There is no
  Bridge but the thread of patience, no way
But the will to wish back Eden, this leaning
  To stand against the persuasions of a wind
That rings with its meaninglessness where it sang its meaning.

Assassin

'The rattle in Trotsky's throat and his wild boar's moans'
                    Piedra de Sol, Octavio Paz

Blood I foresaw. I had put by
  The distractions of the retina, the eye
That like a child must be fed and comforted
  With patterns, recognitions. The room
Had shrunk to a paperweight of glass and he
  To the centre and prisoner of its transparency.

He rasped pages. I knew too well
  The details of that head. I wiped
Clean the glance and saw
  Only his vulnerableness. Under my quivering
There was an ease, save for that starched insistence
  While paper snapped and crackled as in October air.

Sound drove out sight. We inhabited together
  One placeless cell. I must put down
This rage of the ear for discrimination, its absurd
  Dwelling on ripples, liquidities, fact
Fastening on the nerve gigantic paper burrs.
  The gate of history is straiter than eye's or ear's.

In imagination, I had driven the spike
  Down and through. The skull had sagged in its blood.
The grip, the glance – stained but firm –
  Held all at its proper distance and now hold
This autumnal hallucination of white leaves
  From burying purpose in a storm of sibilance.

I strike. I am the future and my blow
  Will have it now. If lightning froze
It would hover as here, the room
  Riding in the crest of the moment's wave,
In the deed's time, the deed's transfiguration
  And as if that wave would never again recede.

The blood wells. Prepared for this
  This I can bear. But papers
Snow to the ground with a whispered roar:
  The voice, cleaving their crescendo, is his
Voice, and his the animal cry
  That has me then by the roots of the hair.

Fleshed in that sound, objects betray me,
  Objects are my judge: the table and its shadow,
Desk and chair, the ground a pressure
  Telling me where it is that I stand
Before wall and window-light:
  Mesh of the curtain, wood, metal, flesh:

A dying body that refuses death,
  He lurches against me in his warmth and weight,
As if my arm's length blow
  Had transmitted and spent its strength
Through blood and bone; and I, spectred,
  The body that rose against me were my own.

Woven from the hair of that bent head,
  The thread that I had grasped unlabyrinthed all –
Tightrope of history and necessity –
  But the weight of a world unsteadies my feet
And I fall into the lime and contaminations
  Of contingency; into hands, looks, time.

Against Extremity

Let there be treaties, bridges,
    Chords under the hands, to be spanned
Sustained: extremity hates a given good
    Or a good gained. That girl who took
Her life almost, then wrote a book
    To exorcize and to exhibit the sin,
Praises a friend there for the end she made
    And each of them becomes a heroine.
The time is in love with endings. The time's
    Spoiled children threaten what they will do,
And those they cannot shake by petulance
    They'll bribe out of their wits by show.
Against extremity, let there be
    Such treaties as only time itself
Can ratify, a bond and test
    Of sequential days, and like the full
Moon slowly given to the night,
    A possession that is not to be possessed.

The Way of a World

Having mislaid it, and then
  Found again in a changed mind
The image of a gull the autumn gust
  Had pulled upwards and past
The window I watched from, I recovered too
  The ash-key, borne-by whirling
On the same surge of air, like an animate thing:
  The scene was there again: the bird,
The seed, the windlines drawn in the sidelong
  Sweep of leaves and branches that only
The black and supple boughs restrained –
  All would have joined in the weightless anarchy
Of air, but for that counterpoise. All rose
  Clear in the memory now, though memory did not choose
Or value it first: it came
  With its worth and, like those tree-tips,
Fine as dishevelling hair, but steadied
  And masted as they are, that worth
Outlasted its lost time, when
  The cross-currents had carried it under.
In all these evanescences of daily air,
  It is the shapes of change, and not the bare
Glancing vibrations, that vein and branch
  Through the moving textures: we grasp
The way of a world in the seed, the gull
  Swayed toiling against the two
Gravities that root and uproot the trees.

Descartes and the Stove

Thrusting its armoury of hot delight,
　　Its negroid belly at him, how the whole
Contraption threatened to melt him
　　Into recognition. Outside, the snow
Starkened all that snow was not –
　　The boughs' nerve-net, angles and gables
Denting the brilliant hoods of it. The foot-print
　　He had left on entering, had turned
To a firm dull gloss, and the chill
　　Lined it with a fur of frost. Now
The last blaze of day was changing
　　All white to yellow, filling
With bluish shade the slots and spoors
　　Where, once again, badger and fox would wind
Through the phosphorescence. All leaned
　　Into that frigid burning, corded tight
By the lightlines as the slow sun drew
　　Away and down. The shadow, now,
Defined no longer: it filled, then overflowed
　　Each fault in snow, dragged everything
Into its own anonymity of blue
　　Becoming black. The great mind
Sat with his back to the unreasoning wind
　　And doubted, doubted at his ear
The patter of ash and, beyond, the snow-bound farms,
　　Flora of flame and iron contingency
And the moist reciprocation of his palms.

On the Principle of Blowclocks

Three-way poem

The static forces
not a ball of silver
of a solid body
but a ball of air
and its material strength
whose globed sheernesses
derive from
shine with a twofold glitter:
not the quantity of mass:
once with the dew and once
an engineer would instance
with the constituent bright threads
rails or T beams, say
of all its spokes
four planes constructed to
in a tense surface
contain the same volume as
in a solid cloud of stars
four tons of mass

A reading of 'On the Principle of Blowclocks' should include (a) the italicized lines, (b) the unitalicized, (c) the whole as printed.

Words for the Madrigalist

Look with the ears, said Orazio Vecchi,
   Trusting to music, willing to be led
Voluntarily blind through its complete
   Landscape of the emotion, feeling beneath the feet
Of the mind's heart, the land fall, the height
   Re-form: Look with the ears – they are all
Looking with the eyes, missing the way:
   So, waiting for sleep, I look
With the ears at the confused clear sounds
   As each replenished tributary unwinds
Its audible direction, and dividing
   The branchwork of chime and counterchime
Runs the river's thick and drumming stem:
   Loud with their madrigal of limestone beds
Where nothing sleeps, they all
   Give back – not the tune the listener calls
But the measure of what he is
   In the hard, sweet music of his lack,
The unpremeditated consonances: and the words
   Return it to you over the ground-
Bass of their syllables, Orazio Vecchi:
   Hear with the eyes as you catch the current of their sounds.

Arroyo Hondo

Twice I'd tried
to pass the
bastard outside
of Arroyo Hondo:
each time, the same
thing: out he
came in a
wobbling glide
in that beat-up
pick-up, his
head bent
in affable accompaniment,
jawing at
the guy who sat
beside him: the third
time (ready
for him) I
cut out wide,
flung him
a passing look as I
made it: we almost
made it together
he and I: the same
thing, out he
came, all crippled speed
unheeding: I could not
retreat and what
did I see? I
saw them
playing at cards
on the driving seat.

A Sense of Distance

The door is shut.
The red rider
no longer crosses the canyon floor
under a thousand feet of air.

The glance that fell
on him, is shafting
a deeper well:
the boughs of the oak are roaring
inside the acorn shell.

The hoofbeats – silent, then –
are sounding now
that ride
dividing a later distance.

For I am in England,
and the mind's embrace
catches-up this English
and that horizonless desert space
into its own, and the three there
concentrically fill a single sphere.

And it seems as if a wind
had flung wide a door
above an abyss, where all
the kingdoms of possibilities shone
like sandgrains crystalline in the mind's own sun.

The Fox Gallery

A long house –
the fox gallery you called
its upper storey, because
you could look down to see
(and did) the way a fox would
cross the field beyond
and you could follow out, window
to window, the fox's way
the whole length of the meadow
parallel with the restraining line
of wall and pane, or as far
as that could follow the sense of all
those windings. Do you remember
the morning I woke you with the cry
Fox fox and the animal
came on – not from side
to side, but straight
at the house and we craned
to see more and more, the most
we could of it and then
watched it sheer off deterred
by habitation, and saw
how utterly the two worlds were
disparate, as that perfect
ideogram for agility
and liquefaction flowed
away from us rhythmical
and flickering and
that flare was final.

To be Engraved on the Skull of a Cormorant

across the thin
façade, the galleried-
with-membrane head:
narrowing, to take
the eye-dividing
declivity where
the beginning beak
prepares for flight
in a still-
perfect salience:
here, your glass
needs must stay
steady and your gross
needle re-tip
itself with reticence
but be
as searching as the sea
that picked and pared
this head yet spared
its frail acuity.

Oppositions

debate with Mallarmé

for Octavio Paz

The poet must rescue etymology from among the footnotes, thus moving up into the body of the text, *'cipher:* the Sanskrit word *sunya* derived from the root *svi*, to swell.'

To cipher is to turn the thought word into flesh. And hence 'the body of the text' derives its substance.

The master who disappeared, taking with him into the echo-chamber the ptyx which the Styx must replenish, has left the room so empty you would take it for fullness.

Solitude charges the house. If all is mist beyond it, the island of daily objects within becomes clarified.

Mistlines flow slowly in, filling the land's declivity that lay unseen until that indistinctness had acknowledged them.

If the skull is a memento mori, it is also a room, whose contained space is wordlessly resonant with the steps that might cross it, to command the vista out of its empty eyes.

Nakedness can appear as the vestment of space that separates four walls, the flesh as certain then and as transitory as the world it shares.

The mind is a hunter of forms, binding itself, in a world that must decay, to present substance.

Skull and shell, both are helmeted, both reconcile vacancy with its opposite. *Abolis bibelots d'inanité sonore.* Intimate presences of silent plenitude.

'Oppositions' replies to one of Mallarmé's most famous sonnets, 'Ses purs ongles très haut dédiant leur onyx', whose 'ptyx' is explained as being a sea shell.

Skullshapes

Skulls. Finalities. They emerge towards new beginnings from undergrowth. Along with stones, fossils, flint keel-scrapers and spoke-shaves, along with bowls of clay pipes heel-stamped with their makers' marks, comes the rural detritus of cattle skulls brought home by children. They are moss-stained, filthy with soil. Washing them of their mottlings, the hand grows conscious of weight, weight sharp with jaggednesses. Suspend them from a nail and one feels the bone-clumsiness go out of them: there is weight still in their vertical pull downwards from the nail, but there is also a hanging fragility. The two qualities fuse and the brush translates this fusion as wit, where leg-like appendages conclude the skulls' dangling mass.

Shadow explores them. It sockets the eye-holes with black. It reaches like fingers into the places one cannot see. Skulls are a keen instance of this duality of the visible: it borders what the eye cannot make out, it transcends itself with the suggestion of all that is there beside what lies within the eyes' possession: it cannot be possessed. Flooded with light, the skull is at once manifest surface and labyrinth of recesses. Shadow reaches down out of this world of helmeted cavities and declares it.

One sees. But not merely the passive mirrorings of the retinal mosaic – nor, like Ruskin's blind man struck suddenly by vision, without memory or conception. The senses, reminded by other seeings, bring to bear on the act of vision their pattern of images; they give point and place to an otherwise naked and homeless impression. It is the mind sees. But what it sees consists not solely of that by which it is confronted grasped in the light of that which it remembers. It sees possibility.

The skulls of birds, hard to the touch, are delicate to the eye. Egg-like in the round of the skull itself and as if the spherical shape were the result of an act like glass-blowing, they resist the eyes' imaginings with the blade of the beak which no lyrical admiration can attenuate to frailty.

The skull of nature is recess and volume. The skull of art – of possibility – is recess, volume and also lines – lines of containment, lines of extension. In seeing, one already extends the retinal impression, searchingly and instantaneously. Brush and pen extend the search beyond the instant, touch discloses a future. Volume, knived across by the challenge of a line, the raggedness of flaking bone countered by ruled, triangular facets, a cowskull opens a visionary field, a play of universals.

The Chances of Rhyme

The chances of rhyme are like the chances of meeting –
   In the finding fortuitous, but once found, binding:
They say, they signify and they succeed, where to succeed
   Means not success, but a way forward
If unmapped, a literal, not a royal succession;
   Though royal (it may be) is the adjective or region
That we, nature's royalty, are led into.
   Yes. We are led, though we seem to lead
Through a fair forest, an Arden (a rhyme
   For Eden) – breeding ground for beasts
Not bestial, but loyal and legendary, which is more
   Than nature's are. Yet why should we speak
Of art, of life, as if the one were all form
   And the other all Sturm-und-Drang? And I think
Too, we should confine to Crewe or to Mow
   Cop, all those who confuse the fortuitousness
Of art with something to be met with only
   At extremity's brink, reducing thus
Rhyme to a kind of rope's end, a glimpsed grass
   To be snatched at as we plunge past it –
Nostalgic, after all, for a hope deferred.
   To take chances, as to make rhymes
Is human, but between chance and impenitence
   (A half-rhyme) come dance, vigilance
And circumstance (meaning all that is there
   Besides you, when you are there). And between
Rest-in-peace and precipice,
   Inertia and perversion, come the varieties
Increase, lease, re-lease (in both
   Senses); and immersion, conversion – of inert
Mass, that is, into energies to combat confusion.
   Let rhyme be my conclusion.

On Water

'Furrow' is inexact:
no ship could be
converted to a plough
travelling this vitreous ebony:

seal it in sea-caves and
you cannot still it:
image on image bends
where half-lights fill it

with illegible depths
and lucid passages,
bestiary of stones,
book without pages:

and yet it confers
as much as it denies:
we are orphaned and fathered
by such solid vacancies:

Stone Speech

Crowding this beach
are milkstones, white
teardrops; flints
edged out of flinthood
into smoothness chafe
against grainy ovals,
pitted pieces, nosestones,
stoppers and saddles;
veins of orange
inlay black beads:
chalk-swaddled babyshapes,
tiny fists, facestones
and facestone's brother
skullstone, roundheads
pierced by a single eye,
purple finds, all
rubbing shoulders:
a mob of grindings,
groundlings, scatterings
from a million necklaces
mined under sea-hills, the pebbles
are as various as the people.

Variation on Paz

Hay que... soñar hacia dentro y tambien hacia afuera

We must dream inwards, and we must dream
   Outwards too, until – the dream's ground
Bound no longer by the dream – we feel
   Behind us the sea's force, and the blind
Keel strikes gravel, grinding
   Towards a beach where, eye by eye,
The incorruptible stones are our witnessess
   And we wake to what is dream and what is real
Judged by the sun and the impartial sky.

The Compact: At Volterra

The crack in the stone, the black filament
    Reaching into the rockface unmasks
More history than Etruria or Rome
    Bequeathed this place. The ramparted town
Has long outlived all that; for what
    Are Caesar or Scipio beside
The incursion of the slow abyss, the daily
    Tribute the dry fields provide

Trickling down? There is a compact
    To undo the spot, between the unhurried sun
Edging beyond this scene, and the moon,
    Risen already, that has stained
Through with its pallor the remaining light:
    Unreal, that clarity of lips and wrinkles
Where shadow investigates each fold,
    Scaling the cliff to the silhouetted stronghold.

Civic and close-packed, the streets
    Cannot ignore this tale of unshorable earth
At the town brink; furrow, gully,
    And sandslide guide down
Each seeping rivulet only to deepen
    The cavities of thirst, dry out
The cenozoic skeleton, appearing, powdering away,
    Uncovering the chapped clay beneath it.

There is a compact between the cooling earth
    And every labyrinthine fault that mines it –
The thousand mouths whose language
    Is siftings, whisperings, rumours of downfall
That might, in a momentary unison,
    Silence all, tearing the roots of sound out
With a single roar: but the cicadas
    Chafe on, grapevine entwines the pergola

Gripping beyond itself. A sole farm
  Eyes space emptily. Those
Who abandoned it still wire
  Their vines between lopped willows:
Their terraces, fondling the soil together,
  Till up to the drop that which they stand to lose:
Refusing to give ground before they must,
  They pit their patience against the dust's vacuity.

The crack in the stone, the black filament
  Rooting itself in dreams, all live
At a truce, refuted, terracing; as if
  Unreasoned care were its own and our
Sufficient reason, to repair the night's derisions,
  Repay the day's delight, here where the pebbles
Of half-ripe grapes abide their season,
  Their fostering leaves outlined by unminding sky.

Ariadne and the Minotaur

When Theseus went down
she stood alone surrounded
by the sense of what finality it was
she entered now: the hot rocks offered her
neither resistance nor escape, but ran
viscous with the image of betrayal:
the pitted and unimaginable face
the minotaur haunted her with
kept forming there
along the seams and discolorations
and in the diamond sweat
of mica: the sword and thread
had been hers to give, and she
had given them, to this easer of destinies:
if she had gone
alone out of the sun and down where he
had threaded the way for her,
if she had gone
winding the ammonite of space
to where at the cold heart
from the dark stone the bestial warmth
would rise to meet her
unarmed in acquiescence, unprepared
her spindle of packthread… her fingers felt now
for the image in the sunlit rock, and her ears
at the shock of touch took up a cry
out of the labyrinth
into their own, a groaning
that filled the stone mouth
hollowly: between the lips of stone
appeared he whom she had sent
to go where her unspeakable
intent unspoken had been to go
herself, and heaved unlabyrinthed at her feet
their mutual completed crime –
a put-by destiny, a dying
look that sought her
out of eyes the light extinguished,

eyes she should have led
herself to light: and the rays
that turned to emptiness in them
filling the whole of space with loss,
a waste of irrefutable sunlight spread
from Crete to Naxos.

'Ariadne and the Minotaur' was suggested initially by Picasso's series of
drawings. It ignores as they do the question of the actual kinship between
Ariadne and the Minotaur. Perhaps she, too, was unaware of it.

Hawks

Hawks hovering, calling to each other
   Across the air, seem swung
Too high on the risen wind
   For the earth-clung contact of our world:
And yet we share with them that sense
   The season is bringing in, of all
The lengthening light is promising to exact
   From the obduracy of March. The pair,
After their kind are lovers and their cries
   Such as lovers alone exchange, and we
Though we cannot tell what it is they say,
   Caught up into their calling, are in their sway,
And ride where we cannot climb the steep
   And altering air, breathing the sweetness
Of our own excess, till we are kinned
   By space we never thought to enter
On capable wings to such reaches of desire.

Autumn Piece

Baffled
by the choreography of the season
the eye could not
with certainty see
whether it was wind
stripping the leaves or
the leaves were struggling to be free:

They came at you
in decaying spirals
plucked flung and regathered by the same
force that was twisting
the scarves of the vapour trails
dragging all certainties out of course:

As the car resisted it
you felt it in either hand
commanding car, tree, sky,
master of chances,
and at a curve was a red
board said 'Danger':
I thought it said dancer.

Event

Nothing is happening
Nothing

A waterdrop
Soundlessly shatters
A gossamer gives

Against this unused space
A bird
Might thoughtlessly try its voice
But no bird does

On the trodden ground
Footsteps
Are themselves more pulse than sound

At the return
A little drunk
On air

Aware that
Nothing
Is happening

The Way In

The needle-point's swaying reminder
  Teeters at thirty, and the flexed foot
Keeps it there. Kerb-side signs
  For demolitions and new detours,
A propped pub, a corner lopped, all
  Bridle the pressures that guide the needle.

I thought I knew this place, this face
  A little worn, a little homely.
But the look that shadows softened
  And the light could grace, keeps flowing away from me
In daily change; its features, rendered down,
  Collapse expressionless, and the entire town

Sways in the fume of the pyre. Even the new
  And mannerless high risers tilt and wobble
Behind the deformations of acrid heat –
  A century's lath and rafters. Bulldozers
Gobble a street up, but already a future seethes
  As if it had waited in the crevices:

A race in transit, a nomad hierarchy:
  Cargoes of debris out of these ruins fill
Their buckled prams: their trucks and hand-carts wait
  To claim the dismantlings of a neighbourhood –
All that a grimy care from wastage gleans,
  From scrap-iron down to heaps of magazines.

Slowing, I see the faces of a pair
  Behind their load: he shoves and she
Trails after him, a sexagenarian Eve,
  Their punishment to number every hair
Of what remains. Their clothes come of their trade –
  They wear the cast-offs of a lost decade.

The place had failed them anyhow, and their pale
   Absorption staring past this time
And dusty space we occupy together,
   Gazes the new blocks down – not built for them;
But what they are looking at they do not see.
   No Eve, but mindless Mnemosyne,

She is our lady of the nameless metals, of things
   No hand has made, and no machine
Has cut to a nicety that takes the mark
   Of clean intention – at best, the guardian
Of all that our daily contact stales and fades,
   Rusty cages and lampless lampshades.

Perhaps those who have climbed into their towers
   Will eye it all differently, the city spread
In unforeseen configurations, and living with this,
   Will find that civility I can only miss – and yet
It will need more than talk and trees
   To coax a style from these disparities.

The needle-point's swaying reminder
   Teeters: I go with uncongealing traffic now
Out onto the cantilevered road, window on window
   Sucked backwards at the level of my wheels.
Is it patience or anger most renders the will keen?
   This is a daily discontent. This is the way in.

At Stoke

I have lived in a single landscape. Every tone
  And turn have had for their ground
These beginnings in grey-black: a land
  Too handled to be primary – all the same,
The first in feeling. I thought it once
  Too desolate, diminished and too tame
To be the foundation for anything. It straggles
  A haggard valley and lets through
Discouraged greennesses, lights from a pond or two.
  By ash-tips, or where the streets give out
In cindery in-betweens, the hills
  Swell up and free of it to where, behind
The whole vapoury, patched battlefield,
  The cows stand steaming in an acrid wind.
This place, the first to seize on my heart and eye,
  Has been their hornbook and their history.

The Marl Pits

It was a language of water, light and air
  I sought – to speak myself free of a world
Whose stoic lethargy seemed the one reply
  To horizons and to streets that blocked them back
In a monotone fume, a bloom of grey.
  I found my speech. The years return me
To tell of all that seasoned and imprisoned:
  I breathe familiar, sedimented air
From a landscape of disembowellings, underworlds
  Unearthed among the clay. Digging
The marl, they dug a second nature
  And water, seeping up to fill their pits,
Sheeted them to lakes that wink and shine
  Between tips and steeples, streets and waste
In slow reclaimings, shimmers, balancings,
  As if kindling Eden rescinded its own loss
And words and water came of the same source.

Class

Those midland *a*'s
once cost me a job:
diction defeated my best efforts –
I was secretary at the time
to the author of *The Craft of Fiction*.
That title was full of class.
You had only to open your mouth on it
to show where you were born
and where you belonged. I tried
time and again I tried
but I couldn't make it
that top *A – ah*
I should say –
it sounded like gargling.
I too visibly shredded his fineness:
it was clear the job couldn't last
and it didn't. Still, I'd always thought him an ass
which he pronounced arse. There's no accounting for taste.

The Rich

I like the rich – the way
they say: 'I'm not made of money':
their favourite pastoral
is to think they're not rich at all –
poorer, perhaps, than you or me,
for they have the imagination of that fall
into the pinched decency
we take for granted. Of course,
they do want to be wanted
by all the skivvies and scrapers
who neither inherited nor rose.
But are they daft or deft,
when they proclaim themselves
men of the left, as if prepared
at the first premonitory flush
of the red dawn
to go rushing onto the street
and, share by share,
add to the common conflagration
their scorned advantage?
They know that it can't happen
in Worthing or Wantage:
with so many safety valves
between themselves and scalding,
all they have to fear
is wives, children, breath and balding.
And at worst
there is always some sunny
Aegean prospect. I like the rich –
they so resemble the rest
of us, except for their money.

After a Death

A little ash, a painted rose, a name.
  A moonshell that the blinding sky
Puts out with winter blue, hangs
  Fragile at the edge of visibility. That space
Drawing the eye up to its sudden frontier
  Asks for a sense to read the whole
Reverted side of things. I wanted
  That height and prospect such as music brings –
Music or memory. Neither brought me here.
  This burial place straddles a green hill,
Chimneys and steeples plot the distances
  Spread vague below: only the sky
In its upper reaches keeps
  An untarnished January colour. Verse
Fronting that blaze, that blade,
  Turns to retrace the path of its dissatisfactions,
Thought coiled on thought, and only certain that
  Whatever can make bearable or bridge
The waste of air, a poem cannot.
  The husk of moon, risking the whole of space,
Seemingly sails it, fraily launched
  To its own death and fullness. We buried
A little ash. Time so broke you down,
  Your lost eyes, dry beneath
Their matted lashes, a painted rose
  Seems both to memorialize and mock
What you became. It picks your name out
  Written on the roll beside a verse –
Obstinate words: measured against the blue,
  They cannot conjure with the dead. Words,
Bringing that space to bear, that air
  Into each syllable we speak, bringing
An earnest to us of the portion
  We must inherit, what thought of that would give
The greater share of comfort, greater fear –
  To live forever, or to cease to live?

The imageless unnaming upper blue
   Defines a world, all images
Of endeavours uncompleted. Torn levels
   Of the land drop, street by street,
Pitted and pooled, its wounds
   Cleansed by a light, dealt out
With such impartiality you'd call it kindness,
   Blindly assuaging where assuagement goes unfelt.

Hyphens

'The country's love-
liness', it said:
what I read was
'the country's love-
lines' – the unnec-
essary 's'
passed over by
the mind's blind-
ly discriminating eye:
but what I saw
was a whole scene
restored: the love-
lines drawing
together the list
'loveliness' capped
and yet left
vague, unloved:
lawns, gardens, houses,
the encircling trees.

Hill Walk

for Philippe and Anne-Marie Jaccottet

Innumerable and unnameable, foreign flowers
   Of a reluctant April climbed the slopes
Beside us. Among them, rosemary and thyme
   Assuaged the coldness of the air, their fragrance
So intense, it seemed as if the thought
   Of that day's rarity had sharpened sense, as now
It sharpens memory. And yet such pungencies
   Are there an affair of every day – Provençal
Commonplaces, like the walls, recalling
   In their broken sinuousness, our own
Limestone barriers, half undone
   By time, and patched against its sure effacement
To retain the lineaments of a place.
   In our walk, time used us well that rhymed
With its own herbs. We crested idly
   That hill of ilexes and savours to emerge
Along the plateau at last whose granite
   Gave on to air: it showed us then
The place we had started from and the day
   Half gone, measured against the distances
That lay beneath, a territory travelled.
   All stretched to the first fold
Of that unending landscape where we trace
   Through circuits, drops and terraces
The outworks, ruinous and overgrown,
   Where space on space has labyrinthed past time:
The unseizable citadel glimmering back at us,
   We contemplated no assault, no easy victory:
Fragility seemed sufficiency that day
   Where we sat by the abyss, and saw each hill
Crowned with its habitations and its crumbled stronghold
   In the scents of inconstant April, in its cold.

Charlotte Corday

O Vertu! le poignard, seul espoir de la terre, Est ton arme sacrée...
                                                              – Chénier

Courteously self-assured, although alone,
With voice and features that could do no hurt,
Why should she not enter? They let in
A girl whose reading made a heroine –
Her book was Plutarch, her republic Rome:
Home was where she sought her tyrant out.

The towelled head next, the huge batrachian mouth:
There was a mildness in him, even. He
Had never been a woman's enemy,
And time and sickness turned his stomach now
From random execution. All the same,
He moved aside to write her victims down,
And when she approached, it was to kill she came.

She struck him from above. One thrust. Her whole
Intent and innocence directing it
To breach through flesh and enter where it must,
It seemed a blow that rose up from within:
Tinville reduced it all to expertise:
– What, would you make of me a hired assassin?

– What did you find to hate in him? – His crimes.
Every reply was temperate save one
And that was human when all's said and done:
The deposition, read to those who sit
In judgement on her, 'What has she to say?'
'Nothing, except that I succeeded in it.'

– You think that you have killed all Marats off?
– I think perhaps such men are now afraid.
The blade hung in its grooves. How should she know
The Terror still to come, as she was led
Red-smocked from gaol out into evening's red?
It was to have brought peace, that faultless blow.

Fouquier Tinville: the public prosecutor.

Uncowed by the unimaginable result,
She loomed by in the cart beneath the eye
Of Danton, Desmoulins and Robespierre,
Heads in a rabble fecund in insult:
She had remade her calendar, called this
The Fourth Day of the Preparation of Peace.

Greater than Brutus was what Adam Lux
Demanded for her statue's sole inscription:
His pamphlet was heroic and absurd
And asked the privilege of dying too:
Though the republic raised to her no statue,
The brisk tribunal took him at his word.

What haunted that composure none could fault?
For she, when shown the knife, had dropped her glance –
She 'who believed her death would raise up France'
As Chénier wrote who joined the later dead:
Her judge had asked: 'If you had gone uncaught,
Would you have then escaped?' 'I would,' she said.

A daggered Virtue, Clio's roll of stone,
Action unsinewed into statuary!
Beneath that gaze what tremor was willed down?
And, where the scaffold's shadow stretched its length,
What unlived life would struggle up against
Death died in the possession of such strength?

Perhaps it was the memory of that cry
That cost her most as Catherine Marat
Broke off her testimony... But the blade
Inherited the future now and she
Entered a darkness where no irony
Seeps through to move the pity of her shade.

Marat Dead

the version of Jacques Louis David

Citoyen, il suffit que je sois bien malheureuse pour avoir droit à votre bienveillance.
Charlotte Corday to Marat

They look like fact, the bath, the wall, the knife,
The splintered packing-case that served as table;
The linen could be priced by any housewife,
As could the weapon too, but not the sable
Suggestion here that colours all we feel
And animates this death-scene from the life
With red, brown, green reflections on the real.

Scaled back to such austerity, each tone
Now sensuous with sadness, would persuade
That in the calm the ugliness has gone
From the vast mouth and from the swaddled head;
And death that worked this metamorphosis
Has left behind no effigy of stone
But wrought an amorous languor with its kiss.

'Citizen, it is enough that I should be
A most unhappy woman to have right
To your benevolence': the heeded plea
Lies on his desk, a patch of bloodied white,
Taking the eye beside the reddening bath,
And single-minded in duplicity,
Loud in the silence of this aftermath.

Words in this painting victimize us all:
Tyro or tyrant, neither shall evade
Such weapons: reader, you grow rational
And miss those sharp intentions that have preyed
On trusting literacy here: unmanned
By generosity and words you fall,
Sprawl forwards bleeding with your pen in hand.

She worked in blood, and paint absolves the man,
And in a bathtub laves all previous stains:
She is the dark and absence in the plan
And he a love of justice that remains.
Who was more deft, the painter or the girl?
Marat's best monument with this began,
That all her presence here's a truthless scrawl.

For Danton

Bound to the fierce Metropolis...
     – Wordsworth, *The Prelude, Book X*

*In the autumn of 1793 – the year in which he had instituted the Revolutionary
Tribunal – Danton went back to his birthplace, Arcis-sur Aube. After his return in
November, he was to be arrested, tried and condemned.*

Who is the man that stands against this bridge
And thinks that he and not the river advances?
Can he not hear the links of consequence
Chiming his life away? Water is time.
Not yet, not yet. He fronts the parapet
Drinking the present with unguarded sense:

The stream comes on. Its music deafens him
To other sounds, to past and future wrong.
The beat is regular beneath that song.
He hears in it a pulse that is his own;
He hears the year autumnal and complete.
November waits for him who has not done

With seeings, savourings. Grape-harvest brings
The south into the north. This parapet
Carries him forward still, a ship from Rheims,
From where, in boyhood and on foot, he'd gone
'To see', he said, 'the way a king is made',
The king that he himself was to uncrown –

Destroyed and superseded, then secure
In the possession of a perfect power
Returned to this: to river, town and plain,
Walked in the fields and knew what power he'd lost,
The cost to him of that metropolis where
He must come back to rule and Robespierre.

Not yet. This contrary perfection he
Must taste into a life he has no time
To live, a lingered, snatched maturity
Before he catches in the waterchime
The measure and the chain a death began,
And fate that loves the symmetry of rhyme
Will spring the trap whose teeth must have a man.

Casarola

for Attilio Bertolucci

Cliffs come sheering down into woodland here:
    The trees – they are chestnuts – spread to a further drop
Where an arm of water rushes through unseen
    Still lost in leaves: you can hear it
Squandering its way towards the mill
    A path crossing a hillslope and a bridge
Leads to at last: the stones lie there
    Idle beside it: they were cut from the cliff
And the same stone rises in wall and roof
    Not of the mill alone, but of shed on shed
Whose mossed tiles like a city of the dead
    Grow green in the wood. There are no dead here
And the living no longer come
    In October to crop the trees: the chestnuts
Dropping, feed the roots they rose from:
    A rough shrine sanctifies the purposes
These doors once opened to, a desolation
    Of still-perfect masonry. There is a beauty
In this abandonment: there would be more
    In the slow activity of smoke
Seeping at roof and lintel; out of each low
    Unwindowed room rising to fill
Full with essences the winter wood
    As the racked crop dried. Waste
Is our way. An old man
    Has been gathering mushrooms. He pauses
To show his spoil, plumped by a soil
    Whose sweet flour goes unmilled:
Rapid and unintelligible, he thinks we follow
    As we feel for his invitations to yes and no:
Perhaps it's the mushrooms he's telling over
    Or this place that shaped his dialect, and where nature
Daily takes the distinctness from that signature
    Men had left there in stone and wood,
Among waning villages, above the cities of the plain.

The Faring

That day, the house was so much a ship
    Clasped by the wind, the whole sky
Piling its cloud-wrack past,
    To be sure you were on dry land
You must go out and stand in that stream
    Of air: the entire world out there
Was travelling too: in each gap the tides
    Of space felt for the earth's ship sides:
Over fields, new-turned, the cry
    And scattered constellations of the gulls
Were messengers from that unending sea, the sky:
    White on brown, a double lambency
Pulsed, played where the birds, intent
    On nothing more than the ploughland's nourishment,
Brought the immeasurable in: wing on wing
    Taking new lustres from the turning year
Above seasonable fields, they tacked and climbed
    With a planet's travelling, rhymed here with elsewhere
In the sea-salt freshnesses of tint and air.

A Night at the Opera

When the old servant reveals she is the mother
   Of the young count whose elder brother
Has betrayed him, the heroine, disguised
   As the Duke's own equerry, sings *Or'*
Che sono, pale from the wound she has received
   In the first act. The entire court
Realize what has in fact occurred and wordlessly
   The waltz song is to be heard now
In the full orchestra. And we, too,
   Recall that meeting of Marietta with the count
Outside the cloister in Toledo. She faints:
   Her doublet being undone, they find
She still has on the hair-shirt
   Worn ever since she was a nun
In Spain. So her secret is plainly out
   And Boccaleone (blind valet
To the Duke) confesses it is he (*Or' son'io*)
   Who overheard the plot to kidnap the dead
Count Bellafonte, to burn by night
   The high camp of the gipsy king
Alfiero, and by this stratagem quite prevent
   The union of both pairs of lovers.
Now the whole cast packs the stage
   Raging in chorus round the quartet – led
By Alfiero (having shed his late disguise)
   And Boccaleone (shock has restored his eyes):
Marietta, at the first note from the count
   (Long thought dead, but finally revealed
As Alfiero), rouses herself, her life
   Hanging by a thread of song, and the Duke,
Descending from his carriage to join in,
   Dispenses pardon, punishment and marriage.
Exeunt to the Grand March, Marietta
   (Though feebly) marching, too, for this
Is the 'Paris' version where we miss
   The ultimate dénouement when at the command
Of the heroine (*Pura non son'*) Bellafonte marries
   The daughter of the gipsy king and

Mushrooms

for Jon and Jill

Eyeing the grass for mushrooms, you will find
A stone or stain, a dandelion puff
Deceive your eyes – their colour is enough
To plump the image out to mushroom size
And lead you through illusion to a rind
That's true – flint, fleck or feather. With no haste
Scent-out the earthy musk, the firm moist white,
And, played-with rather than deluded, waste
None of the sleights of seeing: taste the sight
You gaze unsure of – a resemblance, too,
Is real and all its likes and links stay true
To the weft of seeing. You, to begin with,
May be taken in, taken beyond, that is,
This place of chiaroscuro that seemed clear,
For realer than a myth of clarities
Are the meanings that you read and are not there:
Soon, in the twilight coolness, you will come
To the circle that you seek and, one by one,
Stooping into their fragrance, break and gather,
Your way a winding where the rest lead on
Like stepping stones across a grass of water.

The Gap

It could be that you are driving by.
    You do not need the whole of an eye
To command the thing: the edge
    Of a merely desultory look
Will take it in – it is a gap
    (No more) where you'd expect to see
A field-gate, and there well may be
    But it is flung wide, and the land so lies
All you see is space – that, and the wall
    That climbs up to the spot two ways
To embrace absence, frame skies:
    Why does one welcome the gateless gap?
As an image to be filled with the meaning
    It doesn't yet have? As a confine gone?
A saving grace in so much certainty of stone?
    Reason can follow reason, one by one.
But the moment itself, abrupt
    With the pure surprise of seeing,
Will outlast all after-knowledge and its map –
    Even, and perhaps most then, should the unseen
Gate swing-to across that gap.

In Arden

This is the forest of Arden...

Arden is not Eden, but Eden's rhyme:
    Time spent in Arden is time at risk
And place, also: for Arden lies under threat:
    Ownership will get what it can for Arden's trees:
No acreage of green-belt complacencies
    Can keep Macadam out: Eden lies guarded:
Pardonable Adam, denied its gate,
    Walks the grass in a less-than-Eden light
And whiteness that shines from a stone burns with his fate:
    Sun is tautening the field's edge shadowline
Along the wood beyond: but the contraries
    Of this place are contrarily unclear:
A haze beats back the summer sheen
    Into a chiaroscuro of the heat:
The down on the seeded grass that beards
    Each rise where it meets with sky,
Ripples a gentle fume: a fine
    Incense, smelling of hay smokes by:
Adam in Arden tastes its replenishings:
    Through its dense heats the depths of Arden's springs
Convey echoic waters – voices
    Of the place that rises through this place
Overflowing, as it brims its surfaces
    In runes and hidden rhymes, in chords and keys
Where Adam, Eden, Arden run together
    And time itself must beat to the cadence of this river.

The Shaft

for Guy Davenport

The shaft seemed like a place of sacrifice:
   You climbed where spoil heaps from the hill
Spilled out into a wood, the slate
   Tinkling underfoot like shards, and then
You bent to enter: a passageway:
   Cervix of stone: the tick of waterdrops,
A clear clepsydra: and squeezing through
   Emerged into cathedral space, held-up
By a single rocksheaf, a gerbe
   Buttressing-back the roof. The shaft
Opened beneath it, all its levels
   Lost in a hundred feet of water.
Those miners – dust, beards, mattocks –
   They photographed seventy years ago,
Might well have gone to ground here, pharaohs
   Awaiting excavation, their drowned equipment
Laid-out beside them. All you could see
   Was rock reflections tunneling the floor
That water covered, a vertical unfathomed,
   A vertigo that dropped through centuries
To the first who broke into these fells:
   The shaft was not a place to stare into
Or not for long: the adit you entered by
   Filtered a leaf-light, a phosphorescence,
Doubled by water to a tremulous fire
   And signalling you back to the moist door
Into whose darkness you had turned aside
   Out of the sun of an unfinished summer.

Translating the Birds

The buzzard's two-note cry falls plaintively,
    And, like a seabird's, hesitates between
A mewing, a regret, a plangent plea,
    Or so we must translate it who have never
Hung with the buzzard or above the sea.

It veers a haughty circle with sun-caught breast:
    The small birds are all consternation now,
And do not linger to admire the sight,
    The flash of empery that solar fire
Lends to the predatory ease of flight.

The small birds have all taken to the trees,
    Their eyes alert, their garrulousness gone:
Beauty does not stir them, realists to a man,
    They know what awe's exacted by a king,
They know that now is not the time to sing.

They'll find their way back into song once more
    Who've only sung in metaphor and we
Will credit them with arias, minstrelsy,
    And, eager always for the intelligible,
Instruct those throats what meaning they must tell.

But supply pulsing, wings against the air,
    With yelp that bids the silence of small birds,
Now it is the buzzard owns the sky
    Thrusting itself beyond the clasp of words,
Word to dance with, dally and outfly.

Snow Signs

They say it is waiting for more, the snow
  Shrunk up to the shadow-line of walls
In an arctic smouldering, an unclean salt,
  And will not go until the frost returns
Sharpening the stars, and the fresh snow falls
  Piling its drifts in scallops, furls. I say
Snow has left its own white geometry
  To measure out for the eye the way
The land may lie where a too cursory reading
  Discovers only dip and incline leading
To incline, dip, and misses the fortuitous
  Full variety a hillside spreads for us:
It is written here in sign and exclamation,
  Touched-in contour and chalk-followed fold,
Lines and circles finding their completion
  In figures less certain, figures that yet take hold
On features that would stay hidden but for them:
  Walking, we waken these at every turn,
Waken ourselves, so that our walking seems
  To rouse some massive sleeper out of winter dreams
Whose stretching startles the whole land into life,
  As if it were us the cold, keen signs were seeking
To pleasure and remeasure, repossess
  With a sense in the gathered coldness of heat and height.
Well, if it's for more the snow is waiting
  To claim back into disguisal overnight,
As though it were promising a protection
  From all it has transfigured, scored and bared,
Now we shall know the force of what resurrection
  Outwaits the simplification of the snow.

Their Voices Rang

Their voices rang
through the winter trees:
they were speaking and yet it seemed they sang,
the trunks a hall of victory.

And what is that and where?
Though we come to it rarely,
the sense of all that we might be
conjures the place from air.

Is it the mind, then?
It is the mind received,
assumed into a season
forestial in the absence of all leaves.

Their voices rang
through the winter trees and time
catching the cadence of that song
forgot itself in them.

For Miriam

I

I climbed to your high village through the snow,
    Stepping and slipping over lost terrain:
Wind having stripped a dead field of its white
    Had piled the height beyond: I saw no way
But hung there wrapped in breath, my body beating:
    Edging the drift, trying it for depth,
Touch taught the body how to go
    Through straitest places. Nothing too steep
Or narrow now, once mind and muscle
    Learned to dance their balancings, combined
Against the misdirections of the snow.
    And soon the ground I gained delivered me
Before your smokeless house, and still
    I failed to read that sign. Through cutting air
Two hawks patrolled the reaches of the day,
    Black silhouettes against the sheen
That blinded me. How should I know
    The cold which tempered that blue steel
Claimed you already, for you were old.

II

Mindful of your death, I hear the leap
    At life in the *resurrexit* of Bruckner's mass:
For, there, your hope towers whole:
    Within a body one cannot see, it climbs
That spaceless space, the ear's
    Chief mystery and mind's, that probes to know
What sense might feel, could it outgo
    Its own destruction, spiralling tireless
Like these sounds. To walk would be enough
    And top that rise behind your house
Where the land lies sheer to Wales,
    And Severn's crescent empties and refills
Flashing its sign inland, its pulse
    Of light that shimmers off the Atlantic:

For too long, age had kept you from that sight
   And now it beats within my eye, its pressure
A reply to the vein's own music
   Here, where with flight-lines interlinking
That sink only to twine and hover the higher,
   A circling of hawks recalls to us our chains
And snow remaining hardens above your grave.

III

You wanted a witness that the body
   Time now taught you to distrust
Had once been good. 'My face,' you said –
   And the Shulamite stirred in decembering flesh
As embers fitfully relit – 'My face
   Was never beautiful, but my hair
(It reached then to my knees) was beautiful.'
   We met for conversation, not conversion,
For you were that creature Johnson bridled at –
   A woman preacher. With age, your heresies
Had so multiplied that even I
   A pagan, pleaded for poetry forgone:
You thought the telling-over of God's names
   Three-fold banality, for what you sought
Was single, not (and the flame was in your cheek)
   'A nursery rhyme, a jingle for theologians.'
And the incarnation? That, too, required
   All of the rhetoric that I could bring
To its defence. The frozen ground
   Opened to receive you a slot in snow,
Re-froze, and months unborn now wait
   To take you into the earthdark disincarnate.

IV

A false spring. By noon the frost
   Whitens the shadows only and the stones
Where they lie away from light. The fields
   Give back an odour out of earth
Smoking up through the haysmells where the hay

– I thought it was sunlight in its scattered brightness –
Brings last year's sun to cattle wintering:
   The dark will powder them with white, and day
Discover the steaming herd, as beam
   On beam, and bird by bird, it thaws
Towards another noon. *Et resurrexit*:
   All will resurrect once more,
But whether you will rise again – unless
   To enter the earthflesh and its fullness
Is to rise in the unending metamorphosis
   Through soil and stem… This valediction is a requiem.
What was the promise to Abraham and his seed?
   That they should feed an everlasting life
In earthdark and in sunlight on the leaf
   Beyond the need of hope or help. But we
Would hunger in hope at the shimmer of a straw,
   Although it burned, a mere memory of fire,
Although the beauty of earth were all there were.

V

In summer's heat, under a great tree
   I hear the hawks cry down.
The beauty of earth, the memory of your fire
   Tell of a year gone by and more
Bringing the leaves to light: they spread
   Between these words and the birds that hang
Unseen in predatory flight. Again,
   Your high house is in living hands
And what we were saying there is what was said.
   My body measures the ground beneath me
Warm in this beech-foot shade, my verse
   Pacing out the path I shall not follow
To where you spoke once with a wounded
   And wondering contempt against your flock,
Your mind crowded with eagerness and anger.
   The hawks come circling unappeasably. Their clangour
Seems like the energy of loss. It is hunger.
   It pierces and pieces together, a single note,
The territories they come floating over now:

The escarpment, the foreshore and the sea;
The year that has been, the year to be;
　　Leaf on leaf, a century's increment
That has quickened and weathered, withered on the tree
　　Down into this brown circle where the shadows thicken.

Hay

The air at evening thickens with a scent
That walls exude and dreams turn lavish on –
Dark incense of a solar sacrament
Where, laid in swathes, the field-silk dulls and dries
To contour out the land's declivities
With parallels of grass, sweet avenues:
Scent hangs perpetual above the changes,
As when the hay is turned and we must lose
This clarity of sweeps and terraces
Until the bales space out the slopes again
Like scattered megaliths. Each year the men
Pile them up close before they build the stack,
Leaving against the sky, as night comes on,
A henge of hay-bales to confuse the track
Of time, and out of which the smoking dews
Draw odours solid as the huge deception.

Under the Bridge

Where the ranch-house disappeared its garden
seeded and the narcissi
began through a slow mutation
to breed smaller and smaller stars
unimpaired in scent: beside these
the horns of the cala lilies
each scroll protruding an insistent
yellow pistil seem from their scale
and succulent whiteness to belong
to an earlier world:
if there were men in it the trellises
that brace these stanchions
would fit the scale
of their husbandry and
if they made music it would
shudder and rebound
like that which travels down
the metal to the base
of this giant instrument
bedded among teazle, fennel, grass
in a returning wilderness
under the bridge

San Francisco

San Fruttuoso

the divers

Seasalt has rusted the ironwork trellis
at the one café. Today
the bathers are all sunbathers
and their bodies, side by side,
hide the minute beach:
the sea is rough and the sun's
rays pierce merely fitfully
an ill-lit sky. Unvisited,
the sellers of lace and postcards
have nothing to do, and the Dorias
in their cool tombs under the cloisters
sleep out history unfleshed.
Oggi pesce spada
says the café sign, but we
shall eat no swordfish today:
we leave by the ferry
from which the divers are arriving.
We wait under an orange tree
that produces flowers but no oranges.
They litter the rocks with their gear
and begin to assume
alternative bodies, slipping
into black rubbery skins with *Caution*
written across them.
They are of both sexes. They strap on
waist weights, frog feet,
cylinders of oxygen,
they lean their heaviness which water will lighten
back against rock, resting there
like burdened seals.
They test their cylinders
and the oxygen hisses at them.
They carry knives
and are well equipped to encounter
whatever it is draws them downwards
in their sleek black flesh.
The postcards show Christ –

Cristo del mare –
sunk and standing on his pedestal
with two divers circling
as airy as under-water birds
in baroque, ecstatic devotion
round the bad statue.
Will they find calm down there
we wonder, stepping heavily
over the ship-side gap,
feeling already the unbalancing
pull of the water under us.
We pass the granular rocks
faulted with long scars.
The sea is bristling up to them.
The straightness of the horizon
as we heave towards it
only disguises the intervening
sea-roll and sea-chop, the clutching glitter.
I rather like
the buck of the boat. What I dislike
with the sea tilting at us
is the thought of losing one's brains
as one slides sideways
to be flung at the bulwarks
as if weightless, the 'as if'
dissolving on impact
into bone and blood.
The maternal hand tightens
on the push-chair
that motion is dragging at:
her strapped-in child is asleep.
Perhaps those invisible divers –
luckier than we are –
all weight gone
levitate now
around the statue,
their corps de ballet
like Correggio's sky-
swimming angels, a swarm
of batrachian legs:
they are buoyed up by adoration,

the water merely an accidental aid
to such staggeringly
slow-motion pirouettes
forgetful of body, of gravity.
The sea-lurch snatches
and spins the wheels of his chair
and the child travels the sudden gradient
caught at by other hands,
reversed in mid-flight
and returned across the up-
hill deck to his mother:
a visitor,
she has the placid
and faintly bovine look
of a Northern madonna
and is scarcely surprised; he, too,
stays perfectly collected
aware now of what it was he had forgotten
while sleeping – the stuff
he was chewing from a packet,
which he continues to do.
He has come back to his body once more.
How well he inhabits his flesh:
lordly in unconcern,
he is as well accoutred as those divers.
He rides out the storm chewing and watching,
trustfully unaware
we could well go down –
though we do not, for already
the town is hanging above
us and the calm quay water.
From the roofs up there
perhaps one could see the divers
emerging, immersing,
whatever it is they are at
as we glide forward
up to the solid, deck to dock,
with salted lips.
That same sea
which wrecked Shelley
goes on rocking behind

and within us, hiding
its Christ, its swordfish,
as the coast reveals
a man-made welcome to us
of wall, street, room,
body's own measure and harbour,
shadow of lintel, portal
asking it in.

Above Carrara

for Paolo and Francesco

Climbing to Colonnata past ravines
    Squared by the quarryman, geometric gulfs
Stepping the steep, the wire and gear
    Men use to pare a mountain: climbing
With the eye the absences where green should be,
    The annihilating scree, the dirty snow
Of marble, at last we gained a level
    In the barren flat of a piazza, leaned
And drank from the fountain there a jet
    As cold as tunnelled rock. The place –
Plane above plane and block on block –
    Invited us to climb once more
And, cooled now, so we did
    Deep between church- and house-wall,
Up by a shadowed stairway to emerge
    Where the village ended. As we looked back then
The whole place seemed a quarry for living in,
    And between the acts of quarrying and building
To set a frontier, a nominal petty thing,
    While, far below, water that cooled our thirst
Dyed to a meal now, a sawdust flow,
    Poured down to slake those blades
Slicing inching the luminous mass away
    Above Carrara...

Fireflies

The signal light of the firefly in the rose:
Silent explosions, low suffusions, fire
Of the flesh-tones where the phosphorus touches
On petal and on fold: that close world lies
Pulsing within its halo, glows or goes:
But the air above teems with the circulation
Of tiny stars on darkness, cosmos grows
Out of their circlings that never quite declare
The shapes they seem to pin-point, swarming there
Like stitches of light that fleck and thread a sea,
Yet unlike, too, in that the dark is spaces,
Its surfaces all surfaces seen through,
Discovered depths, filled by a flowering,
And though the rose lie lost now to the eye,
You could suppose the whole of darkness a forming rose.

Instead of an Essay

for Donald Davie

Teacher and friend, what you restored to me
Was love of learning; and without that gift
A cynic's bargain could have shaped my life
To end where it began, in detestation
Of the place and man that had mistaught me.
You were the first to hear my poetry,
Written above a bay in Italy:
Lawrence and Shelley found a refuge once
On that same coast – exiles who had in common
Love for an island slow to learn of it
Or to return that love. And so had we
And do – you from the far shore of the sea
And I beside a stream in Gloucestershire
That feeds it. Meeting maybe once a year
We take the talk up where we left it last,
Forgetful of which fashions, tide on tide –
The Buddha, shamanism, suicide –
Have come and passed.
Brother in a mystery you trace
To God, I to an awareness of delight
I cannot name, I send these lines to you
In token of the prose I did not write.

The Littleton Whale

in memory of Charles Olson

What you wrote to know
was whether
the old ship canal
still paralleled the river
south
of Gloucester (England)…

What I never told
in my reply
was of the morning
on that same stretch
(it was a cold
January day in '85)
when Isobel Durnell
saw the whale…

She was up at dawn
to get her man off on time
to the brickyard and
humping up over the banks
beyond Bunny Row
a slate-grey hill showed
that the night before
had not been there…

They both ran outside
and down to the shore:
the wind was blowing
as it always blows
so hard that the tide
comes creeping up under it
often unheard…

The great grey-blue thing
had an eye
that watched wearily
their miniature motions as they
debated its fate
for the tide
was already feeling beneath it
floating it away...

It was Moses White
master mariner
owner of the sloop Matilda
who said the thing to do
was to get chains and a traction engine
– they got two from Olveston –
and drag it ashore:
the thing was a gift:
before long it would be
drifting off to another part of the coast
and lost to them
if they didn't move now...

And so the whale –
flukes, flesh, tail
trembling no longer
with a failing life –
was chained and hauled
installed above the tideline...

And the crowds came
to where it lay
upside down
displaying a
belly evenly-wrinkled
its eye lost to view
mouth skewed and opening into
an interior of tongue and giant sieves
that had once
filtered that diet of shrimp
its deep-sea sonar

had hunted out for it
by listening to submarine echoes
too slight
for electronic selection...

And Hector Knapp
wrote in his diary:
Thear was a Whal
cum ashore at Littleton Pill
and bid thear a fortnight
He was sixty eaight feet long
His mouth was twelve feet
The Queen claim it at last
and sould it for forty pound
Thear supposed to be
forty thousen pepeal to se it
from all parts of the cuntry...

The Methodist preacher
said that George Sindry
who was a very religious man
told himself when that whale came in
he'd heard so many arguments
about the tale of Jonah not being true
that he went to Littleton to
'satisfy people'. He was a tall man
a six footer
'but I got into that whale's mouth' he said
'and I stood in it
upright...'

The carcass
had overstayed its welcome
so they sent up a sizeable boat
to tow it to Bristol
and put it on show there
before they cut the thing down stinking
to be sold
and spread for manure...

You can still see the sign
to Whale Wharf as they renamed it
and Wintle's Brickworks became
the Whale Brick
Tile and Pottery Works...

Walking daily onto
the now-gone premises
through the 'pasture land
with valuable deposits of clay thereunder'
when the machine- and drying sheds
the five kilns, the stores and stables
stood permanent in that place
of their disappearance
Enoch Durnell still
relished his part in all that history begun
when Bella shook
and woke him with a tale that the tide
had washed up a whole house
with blue slates on it into Littleton Pill
and that house was a whale...

The Flood

It was the night of the flood first took away
    My trust in stone. Perfectly reconciled it lay
Together with water – and does so still –
    In the hill-top conduits that feed into
Cisterns of stone, cisterns echoing
    With a married murmur, as either finds
Its own true note in such a unison.
    It rained for thirty days. Down chimneys
And through doors, the house filled up
    With the roar of waters. The trees were bare,
With nothing to keep in the threat
    And music of that climbing, chiming din
Now rivers ran where the streams once were.
    Daily, we heard the distance lessening
Between house and water-course. But floods
    Occur only along the further plains and we
Had weathered the like of this before
    – The like, but not the equal, as we saw,
Watching it lap the enclosure wall,
    Then topping it, begin to pile across
And drop with a splash like clapping hands
    And spread. It took in the garden
Bed by bed, finding a level to its liking.
    The house-wall, fronting it, was blind
And therefore safe: it was the doors
    On the other side unnerved my mind
– They and the deepening night. I dragged
    Sacks, full of a mush of soil
Dug in the rain, and bagged each threshold.
    Spade in hand, why should I not make
Channels to guide the water back
    Into the river, before my barricade
Proved how weak it was? So I began
    Feeling my way into the moonless rain,
Hacking a direction. It was then as though
    A series of sluices had been freed to overflow
All the land beneath them: it was the dark I dug
    Not soil. The sludge melted away from one

And would not take the form of a trench.
   This work led nowhere, with no bed
To the flood, no end to its sources and resources
   To grow and to go wherever it would
Taking one with it. It was the sound
   Struck more terror than the groundlessness I trod,
The filth fleeing my spade – though that, too,
   Carried its image inward of the dissolution
Such sound orchestrates – a day
   Without reprieve, a swealing away
Past shape and self. I went inside.
   Our ark of stone seemed warm within
And welcoming, yet echoed like a cave
   To the risen river whose tide already
Pressed close against the further side
   Of the unwindowed wall. There was work to do
Here better than digging mud – snatching
   And carrying such objects as the flood
Might seep into, putting a stair
   Between the world of books and water.
The mind, once it has learned to fear
   Each midnight eventuality,
Can scarcely seize on what is already there:
   It was the feet first knew
The element weariness had wandered through
   Eyeless and unreasoning. Awakened eyes
Told that the soil-sacked door
   Still held, but saw then, without looking,
Water had tried stone and found it wanting:
   Wall fountained a hundred jets:
Floor lay awash, an invitation
   To water to follow it deriding door
On door until it occupied the entire house.
   We bailed through an open window, brushing
And bucketing with a mindless fervour
   As though four hands could somehow find
Strength to keep pace, then oversway
   The easy redundance of a mill-race. I say
That night diminished my trust in stone –
   As porous as a sponge, where once I'd seen

The image of a constancy, a ground for the play
    And fluency of light. That night diminished
Yet did not quite betray my trust.
    For the walls held. As we tried to sleep,
And sometimes did, we knew that the flood
    Rivered ten feet beneath us. And so we hung
Between a dream of fear and the very thing.
    Water-lights coursed the brain and sound
Turned it to the tympanum of an ear. When I rose
    The rain had ceased. Full morning
Floated and raced with water through the house,
    Dancing in whorls on every ceiling
As I advanced. Sheer foolishness
    It seemed to pause and praise the shimmer
And yet I did and called you down
    To share this vertigo of sunbeams everywhere,
As if no surface were safe from swaying
    And the very stone were as malleable as clay.
Primeval light undated the day
    Back into origin, washed past stain
And staleness, to a beginning glimmer
    That stilled one's beating ear to sound
Until the flood-water seemed to stream
    With no more burden than the gleam itself.
Light stilled the mind, then showed it what to do
    Where the work of an hour or two could
Hack a bank-side down, let through
    The stream and thus stem half the force
That carried its weight and water out of course.
    Strength spent, we returned. By night
The house was safe once more, but cold within.
    The voice of waters burrowed one's dream
Of ending in a wreck of walls:
    We were still here, with too much to begin
That work might make half-good.
    We waited upon the weather's mercies
And the December stars frosted above the flood.

Above Manhattan

Up in the air
among the Iroquois: no:
they are not born
with a head for heights:
their girder-going
is a learned, at last
a learnèd thing
as sure as instinct:
beneath them
they can see in print
the newssheet of the city
with a single rent where three
columns, clipped out of it,
show the Park was planted:
webbed and cradled
by the catenary
distances of bridge on bridge
the place is as real
as something imaginary:
but from where they are
one must read with care:
for to put
one foot wrong
is to drop
more than a glance
and though
this closeness and that distance
make dancing difficult a dance
it is that the mind is led
above Manhattan

The Iroquois were employed in high construction work.

All Afternoon

All afternoon the shadows have been building
A city of their own within the streets,
Carefully correcting the perspectives
With dark diagonals, and paring back
Sidewalks into catwalks, strips of bright
Companionways, as if it were a ship
This counter-city. But the leaning, black
Enjambements like ladders for assault
Scale the façades and tie them to the earth,
Confounding fire-escapes already meshed
In slatted ambiguities. You touch
The sliding shapes to find which place is which
And grime a finger with the ash of time
That blows through both, the shadow in the shade
And in the light, that scours each thoroughfare
To pit the walls, rise out of yard and stairwell
And tarnish the Chrysler's Aztec pinnacle.

At the Trade Center

Paused at the more than Brocken summit,
    Hand outstretched to touch and cover
The falling height beneath, I watch
    Between the nakedness of fingers – light
On each knuckled promontory of flesh
    And shadows tremulous between the gaps –
The map of land, the map of air:
    Rivers both sides of this island
Tug the gaze askance from the grid of streets
    To the sea- and bird-ways, the expanse
That drinks the reverberation of these energies.
    What can a hand bring back into a view
No rule of thumb made possible? It spans
    The given rigours and the generous remissions
Of ocean, of the ferryings to-and-fro
    Between the harbour and the islands. As you climb
The more you see of waters and of marsh
    Where, angle-poised, the heron
Stands within earshot of this city
    Back to the horizon, studying its pool.
The horizon is where we are:
    The Bridge is small from this new vantage,
The view in space become a view in time:
    Climbing we see an older city's fall –
The waterfront is down: the clerks are hived
    Window on window where the town began
And spread. I spread my fingers
    And the traffic runs between. The elevator grounds
Us back to streets where in the cracks
    Between immeasurable buildings beggars
From their domains of dust and paper-bags
    Hold out one hand deep in the traffic sounds.

To Ivor Gurney

Driving north, I catch the hillshapes, Gurney,
   Whose drops and rises – Cotswold and Malvern
In their cantilena above the plains –
   Sustained your melody: your melody sustains
Them, now – Edens that lay
   Either side of this interminable roadway.
You would recognize them still, but the lanes
   Of lights that fill the lowlands, brim
To the Severn and glow into the heights.
   You can regain the gate: the angel with the sword
Illuminates the paths to let you see
   That night is never to be restored
To Eden and England spangled in bright chains.

Black Brook

Black Brook is brown. It travels
   With the hillside in it – an upside-down
Horizon above a brackened slope – until
   It drops and then: rags and a rush of foam
Whiten the peat-stained stream
   That keeps changing note and singing
The song of its shingle, its shallowness or its falls.
   I pace a parallel track to that of the water:
It must be the light of a moorland winter
   Let them say that black was fair name
For such a stream, making it mirror
   Solely the granite and the grey
As no doubt it can. But look! Black Brook
   Has its horizon back, and a blue
Inverted sky dyeing it through to a bed
   Of dazzling sand, an ore of gravel
It has washed out beneath rock and rowan
   As it came here homing down
To the valley it brightens belying its name.

Poem for my Father

I bring to countryside my father's sense
Of an exile ended when he fished his way
Along the stained canal and out between
The first farms, the uninterrupted green,
To find once more the Suffolk he had known
Before the Somme. Yet there was not one tree
Unconscious of that name and aftermath
Nor is there now. For everything we see
Teaches the time that we are living in,
Whose piecemeal speech the vocables of Eden
Pace in reminder of the full perfection,
As oaks above these waters keep their gold
Against the autumn long past other trees
Poised between paradise and history.

The Beech

Blizzards have brought down the beech tree
   That, through twenty years, had served
As landmark or as limit to our walk:
   We sat among its roots when buds
Fruitlike in their profusion tipped the twigs –
   A galaxy of black against a sky that soon
Leaf-layers would shut back. The naked tree
   Commanded, manned the space before it
And beyond, dark lightnings of its branches
   Played above the winter desolation:
It seemed their charge had set the grass alight
   As a low sun shot its fire into the valley
Splitting the shadows open. Today that sun
   Shows you the place uncitadelled,
A wrecked town centred by no spire,
   Scattered and splintered wide. At night
As the wind comes feeling for those boughs
   There is nothing now in the dark of an answering strength,
No form to confront and to attest
   The amplitude of dawning spaces as when
The tower rebuilt itself out of the mist each morning.

Night Fishers

After the autumn storms, we chose a night
    To fish the bay. The catch
I scarcely recollect. It was the climb,
    The grasp at slipping rock unnerved
All thought, thrust out of time
    And into now the sharp original fear
That mastered me then. I do not think
    I ever looked so far down into space
As through the clefts we over-leapt:
    Beams of our torches given back
Off walls and water in each rift
    Crossed and recrossed one another, so the mind
Recalling them, still seems to move
    Inside a hollow diamond that the dark
As shadows shift, threatens to unfacet:
    It was no jewel, it was the flesh would shatter.
And yet it did not. Somehow we arrived
    And crouched there in the cool. The night
Save for the whispered water under-cliff,
    The hiss of falling casts, lay round
Thick with silence. It seemed
    A sky spread out beneath us, constellations
Swimming into view wherever fish
    Lit up its dark with phosphor. A thousand
Points of light mapped the expanse
    And depth, and yet the cliff-top height
Hinted no pull of vertigo along
    Its sudden edge: through diaphanous waters
The radium in the flowing pitchblende glowed
    Holding both mind and eye
Encompassed by a stir of scattered lambency:
    And unalarmed, I could forget
As night-bound we fished on unharmed,
    The terrors of the way we'd come, put by
The terrors of return past fault and fall,
    Watching this calm firmament of the sea.

The Sound of Time

When the clock-tick fades
out of the ear you
can listen to time
in the flow of fire:

and there a cascade
streams up the coals:
loud as Niagara
these climbing falls:

it pours within
forked and fleering
over the thresholds
of a deafened hearing

till the superfluity
of the room's recess
has filled the auricle
with time's abyss

In the Borghese Gardens

for Attilio Bertolucci

Edging each other towards consummation
On the public grass and in the public eye,
Under the Borghese pines the lovers
Cannot tell what thunderheads mount the sky,
To mingle with the roar of afternoon
Rumours of the storm that must drench them soon.

Cars intersect the cardinal's great dream,
His parterres redesigned, gardens half-gone,
Yet Pluto's grasp still bruises Proserpine,
Apollo still hunts Daphne's flesh in stone,
Where the Borghese statuary and trees command
The ever-renewing city from their parkland.

The unbridled adolescences of gods
Had all of earth and air to cool their flights
And to rekindle. But where should lovers go
These torrid afternoons, these humid nights
While Daphne twists in leaves, Apollo burns
And Proserpine returns, returns, returns?

Rome is still Rome. Its ruins and its squares
Stand sluiced in wet and all its asphalt gleaming,
The street fronts caged behind the slant of rain-bars
Sun is already melting where they teem:
Spray-haloed traffic taints your laurel leaves,
City of restitutions, city of thieves.

Lovers, this giant hand, half-seen, sustains
By lifting up into its palm and plane
Our littleness: the shining causeway leads
Through arches, bridges, avenues and lanes
Of stone, that brought us first to this green place –
Expelled, we are the heirs of healing artifice.

Deserted now, and all that callow fire
Quenched in the downpour, here the parkland ways
Reach out into the density of dusk,
Between an Eden lost and promised paradise,
That overbrimming scent, rain-sharpened, fills,
Girdled within a rivercourse and seven hills.

In San Clemente

What deer are these stand drinking at the spring?
Ask of the child the saint is carrying
Across a stream in spate. The steps that flow
Downwards through the sonorous dark beneath,
Should be a water-stair, for where they go,
A child that angels bring forth on the wall
Has lived a whole year on the ocean bed;
Then, down once more, and past the humid cave
Of Mithras' bull and shrine, until they lead
To a wall of tufa and – beyond – the roar
Of subterranean waters pouring by
All of the centuries it takes to climb
From Mithras to the myth-resisting play
Of one clear jet chiming against this bowl
In the fountained courtyard and the open day.

The Return

to Paolo Bertolani

I *The Road*

I could not draw a map of it, this road,
Nor say with certainty how many times
It doubles on itself before it climbs
Clear of the ascent. And yet I know
Each bend and vista and could not mistake
The recognitions, the recurrences
As they occur, nor where. So my forgetting
Brings back the track of what was always there
As new as a discovery. And now
The summit gives us all that lies below,
Shows us the islands slide into their places
Beyond the shore and, when the lights come on,
How all the other roads declare themselves
Garlanding their gradients to the sea,
How the road that brought us here has dropped away
A half-lost contour on a chart of lights
The waters ripple and spread across the bay.

II *Between Serra and Rocchetta*

Walking to La Rocchetta, thirty years
Would not be long enough to teach the mind
Flower by flower their names and their succession.
Walking to La Rocchetta, leave behind
The road, the fortress and the radar tower
And turn across the hill. From thirty years
I have brought back the image to the place.
The place has changed, the image still remains –
A spot that, niched above a half-seen bay,
Climbs up to catch the glitter from beyond
Of snow and marble off the Apennines.
But where are the walls, the wells, the living lines
That led the water down from plot to plot?

Hedges have reached the summits of the trees
Over the reeds and brambles no one cut.
When first I came, it was a time of storms:
Grey seas, uneasily marbling, scourged the cliff:
The waters had their way with skiff on skiff
And, beached, their sides were riven against stone,
Or, anchored, rode the onrush keels in air
Where hope and livelihood went down as one.
Two things we had in common, you and I
Besides our bitterness at want of use,
And these were poetry and poverty:
This was a place of poverty and splendour:
All unprepared, when clarity returned
I felt the sunlight prise me from myself
And from the youthful sickness I had learned
As shield from disappointments: cure came slow
And came, in part, from what I grew to know
Here on this coast among its reefs and islands.
I looked to them for courage across time,
Their substance shaped itself to mind and hand –
Severe the grace a place and people share
Along this slope where Serra took its stand:
For years I held those shapes in thought alone,
Certain you must have left long since, and then
Returning found that you had never gone.
What is a place? For you a single spot.
Walking to La Rocchetta we can trace
In all that meets the eye and all that does not
Half of its history, the other lies
In the rise, the run, the fall of voices:
Innumerable conversations chafe the air
At thresholds and in alleys, street and square
Of those who climbed this slope to work its soil,
And phrases marrying a tongue and time
Coil through the mind's ear, climbing now with us
Through orchids and the wild asparagus:
For place is always an embodiment
And incarnation beyond argument,
Centre and source where altars, once, would rise
To celebrate those lesser deities

We still believe in – angels beyond fable
Who still might visit the patriarch's tent and table
Both here and now, or rather let us say
They rustle through the pages you and I
Rooted in earth, have dedicated to them.
Under the vines the fireflies are returning:
Pasolini spoke of their extinction.
Our lookout lies above a poisoned sea:
Wrong, he was right, you tell us – I agree,
Of one thing the enigma is quite sure,
We have lived into a time we shall not cure.
But climbing to La Rocchetta, let there be
One sole regret to cross our path today,
That she, who tempered your beginning pen
Will never take this road with us again
Or hear, now, the full gamut of your mastery.

III Graziella

We cannot climb these slopes without our dead;
We need no fiction of a hillside ghosted,
A fade-out on the tremor of the sea.
The dead do not return, and nor shall we
To pry and prompt the living or rehearse
The luxuries of self-debating verse.
Their silence we inhabit now they've gone
And like a garment drawn the darkness on
Beyond all hurt. This quiet we must bear:
Put words into their mouths, you fail to hear
What once they said. I can recall the day
She imitated my clipped, foreign way
Of saying *Shakespeare*: English, long unheard,
Came flying back, some unfamiliar bird
Cutting a wing-gust through the weight of air
As she repeated it – *Shakespeare Shakespeare* –
Voice-prints of a season that belongs
To the cicadas and the heat, their song
Shrill, simmering and continuous.
Why does a mere word seem autonomous

We catch back from the grave? The wave it rides
Was spent long-since, dissolved within the tides
Of space and time. And yet the living tone
Shaped to that sound, and mocking at its own,
A voice at play, amused, embodied, clear,
Spryer than any ghost still haunts the ear.
The dog days, the cicada had returned
And through that body more than summer burned
A way and waste into its dark terrain,
Burned back and back till nothing should remain,
Yet could not dry the mind up at its source:
Clear as her voice-print, its unyielded force
Would not be shadowed out of clarity
Until the moment it had ceased to be.
Downhill, between the olives, more than eye
Must tell the foot what path it travels by;
The sea-lights' constellations sway beneath
And we are on the Easter side of death.

IV *The Fireflies*

I have climbed blind the way down through the trees
(How faint the phosphorescence of the stones)
On nights when not a light showed on the bay
And nothing marked the line of sky and sea –
Only the beating of the heart defined
A space of being in the faceless dark,
The foot that found and won the path from blindness,
The hand, outstretched, that touched on branch and bark.
The soundless revolution of the stars
Brings back the fireflies and each constellation,
And we are here half-shielded from that height
Whose star-points feed the white lactation, far
Incandescence where the single star
Is lost to sight. This is a waiting time.
Those thirty, lived-out years were slow to rhyme
With consonances unforeseen, and, gone,
Were brief beneath the seasons and the sun.
We wait now on the absence of our dead,

Sharing the middle world of moving lights
Where fireflies taking torches to the rose
Hover at those clustered, half-lit porches,
Eyelid on closed eyelid in their glow
Flushed into flesh, then darkening as they go.
The adagio of lights is gathering
Across the sway and counter-lines as bay
And sky, contrary in motion, swerve
Against each other's patternings, while these
Tiny, travelling fires gainsay them both,
Trusting to neither empty space nor seas
The burden of their weightless circlings. We,
Knowing no more of death than other men
Who make the last submission and return,
Savour the good wine of a summer's night
Fronting the islands and the harbour bar,
Uncounted in the sum of our unknowings
How sweet the fireflies' span to those who live it,
Equal, in their arrivals and their goings,
With the order and the beauty of star on star.

Catacomb

A Capuchin – long acquaintance with the dead
    Has left him taciturn – stands guard
At gate and stairhead. Silent, he awaits
    The coin we drop into his dish, and then
Withdraws to contemplation – though his eye
    Glides with a marvellous economy sideways
Towards the stair, in silent intimation
    You may now descend. We do – and end up
In a corridor with no end in view: dead
    Line the perspective left and right
Costumed for resurrection. The guidebook had not lied
    Or tidied the sight away – and yet
Eight thousand said, unseen, could scarcely mean
    The silence throughout this city of the dead,
Street on street of it calling into question
    That solidity the embalmer would counterfeit.
Mob-cap, cape, lace, stole and cowl,
    Frocked children still at play
In the Elysian fields of yesterday
    Greet each morning with a morning face
Put on a century ago. Why are we here? –
    Following this procession, bier on bier
(The windowed dead, within), and those
    Upright and about to go, but caught
Forever in their parting pose, as though
    They might have died out walking. Some
Face us from the wall, like damaged portraits;
    Some, whose clothing has kept its gloss,
Glow down across the years at us
    Why are you here? And why, indeed,
For the sunlight through a lunette overhead
    Brightens along a sinuous bole of palm:
Leaves catch and flare it into staring green
    Where a twine of tendril sways inside
Between the bars. Light from that sky
    Comes burning off the bay
Vibrant with Africa; in public gardens
    Tenses against the butterflies' descent

The stamens of red hibiscus. Dead
    Dressed for the promenade they did not take,
Are leaning to that light: it is the sun
    Must judge them, for the sin
Of vanity sits lightly on them: it is the desire
    To feel its warmth against the skin
Has set them afoot once more in this parade
    Of epaulette, cockade and crinoline. We are here
Where no northern measure can undo
    So single-minded a lure – if once a year
The house of the dead stood open
    And these, dwelling beneath its roof,
Were shown the world's great wonders,
    They would marvel beyond every other thing
At the sun. Today, the dead
    Look out from their dark at us
And keep their counsel. The Capuchin
    Has gone off guard, to be replaced
By a brother sentry whose mind is elsewhere –
    Averted from this populace whose conversion
Was nominal after all. His book
    Holds fast his eyes from us. His disregard
Abolishes us as we pass beyond the door.

Palermo

In Memory of George Oppen

We were talking of O'Hara.
'Difficult', you said
'to imagine a good death – *he died*
quietly in bed, in place of:
he was run down
by a drunk.' And now, your own.
First, the long unskeining year by year
of memory and mind. You 'seemed
to be happy' is all I hear.
A lost self does not hide:
what seemed happy was not you
who died before you died. And yet
out of nonentity, where did the words
spring from when
towards the end you told
your sister, 'I don't know
if you have anything to say
but let's take out all the adjectives
and we'll find out' – the way,
lucidly unceremonious,
you spoke to her in life and us.

At Huexotla

Tall on its mound, el Paupérrimo –
the poorest
church in Mexico
and the smallest.

It was not the sight
but the sound of the place
caused us to quicken our step
across the intervening space

between us and it –
such skeins, scales, swells
came from each bell-tower
though not from bells.

Who would compose
a quartet for flutes? – and yet
that was the music
rose to assail us.

A minute interior:
sun on the gold:
flute-timbre on flute
still unfolded there.

Flanking the altar,
caged birds hung,
the alchemy of light transmuting
gold to song:

for it was the light's
reflection had set
those cages in loud accord
and only night would staunch it.

A Rose for Janet

I know
this rose is only
an ink-and-paper rose
but see how it grows and goes
on growing
beneath your eyes:
a rose in flower
has had (almost) its vegetable hour
whilst my
rose of spaces and typography
can reappear at will
(your will)
whenever you repeat
this ceremony of the eye
from the beginning
and thus
learn how
to resurrect a rose
that's instantaneous
perennial
and perfect now

Ararat

We shall sleep-out together through the dark
The earth's slow voyage across centuries
Towards whatever Ararat its ark
Is steering for. Our atoms then will feel
The jarring and arrival of that keel
In timelessness, and rise through galaxies,
Motes starred by the first and final light to show
Whether those shores are habitable or no.

Annunciation

The cat took fright
at the flashing wing of sunlight
as the thing
entered the kitchen, angel of appearances,
and lingered there.

What was it the sun
had sent to say
by his messenger, this solvent ray,
that charged and changed
all it looked at, narrowing even the eye of a cat?

Utensils caught a shine
that could not be used, utility
unsaid by this invasion
from outer space, this gratuitous occasion
of unchaptered gospel.

'I shall return,' the appearance promised,
'I shall not wait for the last
day – every day
is fortunate even when you catch
my ray only as a gliding ghost.

What I foretell
is the unaccountable birth each time
my lord the light, a cat and you
share this domestic miracle:
it asks the name anew

of each thing named
when an earlier, shining dispensation
reached down into mist
and found the solidity
these windows and these walls surround,

and where each cup,
dish, hook and nail
now gathers and guards the sheen
drop by drop
still spilling-over
out of the grail of origin.'

The Plaza

People are the plot
and what they do here –
which is mostly sit
or walk through. The afternoon sun
brings out the hornets:
they dispute with no one, they too
are enjoying their ease
along the wet brink of the fountain,
imbibing peace and water
until a child arrives,
takes off his shoe
and proceeds methodically
to slaughter them. He has the face
and the ferocious concentration
of one of those Aztec gods
who must be fed on blood.
His mother drags him away, half-shod,
and then puts back the shoe
over a dusty sock.
Some feet go bare, some sandalled,
like these Indians who march through
– four of them – carrying a bed
as if they intended to sleep here.
Their progress is more brisk
than that of the ants at our feet
who are removing – some
by its feelers, some
supporting it on their backs –

a dead moth
as large as a bird.
As the shadows densen
in the gazebo-shaped bandstand
the band are beginning to congregate.
The air would be tropical
but for the breath of the sierra:
it grows opulent on the odour
of jacaranda and the turpentine
of the shoeshine boys
busy at ground-level,
the squeak of their rags on leather
 like an angry, repeated bird-sound.
The conductor rises,
flicks his score with his baton –
moths are circling the bandstand light –
and sits down after each item.
The light falls onto the pancakes
of the flat military hats
that tilt and nod
as the musicians under them
converse with one another – then,
the tap of the baton. It must be
the presence of so many flowers enriches the brass:
tangos take on a tragic air,
but the opaque scent
makes the modulation into waltz-time seem
an invitation – not to the waltz merely –
but to the thought that there may be
the choice (at least for the hour)
of dying like Carmen
then rising like a flower.
A man goes by, carrying a fish
that is half his length
wrapped in a sheet of plastic
but nobody sees him. And nobody hears
the child in a torn dress
selling artificial flowers,
mouthing softly in English, 'Flowerrs'.
High heels, bare feet

around the tin cupola of the bandstand
patrol to the beat of the band:
this is the democracy
of the tierra templada – a contradiction
in a people who have inherited
so much punctilio, and yet
in all the to-and-fro
there is no frontier set:
the shopkeepers, the governor's sons,
the man who is selling balloons
in the shape of octopuses, bandannaed heads
above shawled and suckled children
keep common space
with a trio of deaf mutes
talking together in signs,
all drawn to the stir
of this rhythmic pulse
they cannot hear. The musicians
are packing away their instruments:
the strollers have not said out their say
and continue to process
under the centennial trees.
A moon has worked itself free
of the excluding boughs
above the square, and stands
unmistily mid-sky, a precisionist.
The ants must have devoured their prey by this.
As for the fish… three surly Oaxaqueños
are cutting and cooking it
to feed a party of French-speaking Swiss
at the Hotel Calesa Real.
The hornets that failed to return
stain the fountain's edge,
the waters washing and washing away at them,
continuing throughout the night
their whisperings of ablution
where no one stirs,
to the shut flowerheads and the profuse stars.

Oaxaca

The House in the Quarry

What is it doing there, this house in the quarry?
    On the scrap of a height it stands its ground:
The cut-away cliffs rise round it
    And the dust lies heavy along its sills.
Still lived in? It must be, with the care
    They have taken to train its vine
Whose dusty pergola keeps back the blaze
    From a square of garden. Can it be melons
They are growing, a table someone has set out there
    As though, come evening, you might even sit at it
Drinking wine? What dusty grapes
    Will those writhen vine-stocks show for the rain
To cleanse in autumn? And will they taste then
    Of the lime-dust of this towering waste,
Or have transmuted it to some sweetness unforeseen
    That original cleanliness could never reach
Rounding to insipidity? All things
    Seem possible in this unreal light –
The poem still to be quarried here,
    The house itself lit up to repossess
Its stolen site, as the evening matches
    Quiet to the slowly receding thunder of the last
Of the lorries trundling the unshaped marble down and past.

At the Autumn Equinox

for Giuseppe Conte

Wild boars come down by night
 Sweet-toothed to squander a harvest
In the vines, tearing apart
 The careful terraces whose clinging twines
Thicken out to trunks and seem
 To hold up the pergolas they embrace.
Make fast the gate. Under a late moon
 That left the whole scene wild and clear,
I came on twenty beasts, uprooting, browsing
 Here these ledges let into the hillside.
They had undone and taken back again
 Into their nomad scavengers' domain
All we had shaped for use, and laid it waste
 In a night's carouse. Which story is true?
Those who are not hunters say that hunters brought
 The beasts to this place, to multiply for sport
And that they bred here, spread. Or should one credit
 The tale told of that legendary winter
A century since, which drove them in starving bands
 Out from the frozen heartlands of the north?
Ice had scabbed every plane and pine,
 Tubers and roots lay slabbed beneath the ground
That nothing alive or growing showed above
 To give promise of subsistence. They drove on still
Until they found thickets greening up through snow
 And ate the frozen berries from them. Then
Down to the lowland orchards and the fields
 Where crops rooted and ripened. Or should one
Go back to beginnings and to when
 No men had terraced out these slopes? Trees
Taller than the oaks infested then
 These rocks now barren, their lianas
Reaching to the shore – the shore whose miles
 On miles of sand saw the first approach
As swarms swam inland from the isles beyond
 And took possession. Are these

The remnant of that horde, forsaking forests
  And scenting the orchards in their wake? I could hear them
Crunch and crush a whole harvest
  From the vines while the moon looked on.
A mouse can ride on a boar's back,
  Nest in its fur, gnaw through the hide and fat
And not disturb it, so obtuse is their sense of touch –
  But not of sight or smell. I stood
Downwind and waited. It takes five dogs
  To hunt a boar. I had no gun
Nor, come to that, the art to use one:
  I was man alone: I had no need
Of legends to assure me how strange they were –
  A sufficiency of fear confessed their otherness.
Stay still I heard the heartbeats say:
  I could see all too clear
In the hallucinatory moonlight what was there.
  Day led them on. Next morning found
These foragers on ground less certain
  Than dug soil or the gravel-beds
Of dried-up torrents. Asphalt
  Confused their travelling itch, bemused
And drew them towards the human outskirts.
  They clattered across its too-smooth surfaces –
Too smooth, yet too hard for those snouts
  To root at, or tusks to tear out
The rootage under it. Its colour and its smell,
  The too-sharp sunlight, the too-tepid air
Stupified the entire band: water
  That they could swim, snow that had buried
All sustenance from them, worried them far less
  Than this man-made ribbon luring them on
Helpless into the shadow of habitation.
  The first building at the entrance to the valley
Had *Carabinieri* written across its wall:
  Challenged, the machine-gunned law
Saw to it with one raking volley
  And brought the procession to the ground,
Then sprayed it again, to put beyond all doubt
  That this twitching confusion was mostly dead

And that the survivors should not break out
    Tusked and purposeful to defend themselves.
Blood on the road. A crowd, curious
    To view the end of this casual hecatomb
And lingeringly inspect what a bullet can do.
    It was like the conclusion of all battles.
Who was to be pitied and who praised?
    Above the voices, the air hung
Silent, cleared, by the shots, of birdsong
    And as torn into, it seemed, as the flesh below.
Quietly now, at the edges of the crowd,
    Hunters looked the disdain they felt
For so unclean a finish, and admired
    The form those backs, subdued, still have,
Lithe as the undulation of a wave. The enemy
    They had seen eviscerate a dog with a single blow
Brought into the thoughts of these hunters now
    Only their poachers' bitterness at flesh foregone
As their impatience waited to seize on the open season,
    The autumn equinox reddening through the trees.

The Butterflies

They cover the tree and twitch their coloured capes,
    On thin legs, stalking delicately across
The blossoms breathing nectar at them;
    Hang upside-down like bats,
Like wobbling fans, stepping, tipping,
    Tipsily absorbed in what they seek and suck.
There is a bark-like darkness
    Of patterned wrinklings as though of wood
As wings shut against each other.
    Folded upon itself, a black
Cut-out has quit the dance;
    One opens, closes from splendour into drab,
Intent antennae preceding its advance
    Over a floor of flowers. Their skeletons
Are all outside – fine nervures
    Tracing the fourfold wings like leaves;
Their mouths are for biting with – they breathe
    Through stigmata that only a lens can reach:
The faceted eyes, a multiplying glass
    Whose intricacies only a glass can teach,
See us as shadows if they see at all.
    It is the beauty of wings that reconciles us
To these spindles, angles, these inhuman heads
    Dipping and dipping as they sip.
The dancer's tread, the turn, the pirouette
    Come of a choreography not ours,
Velvets shaken out over flowers on flowers
    That under a thousand (can they be felt as) feet
Dreamlessly nod in vegetative sleep.

Chance

I saw it as driving snow, the spume,
    Then, as the waves hit rock
Foam-motes took off like tiny birds
    Drawn downwind in their thousands
Coiled in its vortices. They settled
    Along ledges and then fell back,
Condensed on the instant at the touch of stone
    And slid off, slicking the rock-sides
As they went. The tide went, too,
    Dragging the clicking pebbles with it
In a cast of chattering dice. What do they tell
    These occurrences, these resemblances that speak to you
With no human voice? What they told then
    Was that the energies pouring through space and time,
Spun into snow-lace, suspended into flight,
    Had waited on our chance appearance here,
To take their measure, to re-murmur in human sounds
    The nearing roar of this story of far beginnings
As it shapes out and resounds itself along the shore.

Paris in Sixty-Nine

for Octavio Paz

'I love', I heard you say,
   'To walk in the morning.' We were walking,
Spring light sharpening each vista,
   Under the symmetrical, freshly-leafing trees,
By boulevard, bridge and quays the Douanier
   Had painted into his golden age
Of a Tour Eiffel perpetually new.
   I replied: 'I trust the thoughts that come to me
When walking. Do you, too, *work* when walking?'
   'Work when I am working...?' My error
(Traffic was too loud to fight with words)
   Came clear to me at last – for I
Am far too fast imagining that my friends
   Prefer, like me, the stir of street or landscape
To four walls to work in. Sunlight
   Had begun, after a night of frost, to warm
The April air to temperate perfection,
   In which the mathematics of sharp shade
Would have gratified Le Nôtre, 'auteur de ce jardin':
   His bust surveyed it: in the pavilion there
The subtler geometries of Cézanne. Refaire
   Poussin après la nature! – he and the auteur
Might have seen eye to eye, perhaps,
   But for the straight lines and the grandeur.
All was not easy here. Gendarmerie
   Clustered at corners, still unrelenting
After the late events, although the theatre
   Deserted by its actors now, lay silent
But for the sloganned walls. 'De Gaulle', I said,
   'Is an unpleasant man.' 'But a great one,'
You replied, to my surprise, for you
   Believed when the students had their Day
It was a sign that linearity
   Was coming to its close, and time
Was circling back to recurrence and fiesta.
   Before the walker the horizon slips from sight.

What matters in the end (it never comes)
    Is what is seen along the way.
Our feet now found confronting us
    The equestrian bulk ('Paris vaut une messe!')
Of Henri Quatre in the Place Dauphine,
    Horsed on the spot that Breton called
'The sex of Paris', legs of roadways
    Straddling out from it. Was it the image
Drew him to that statue, or had he
    (Eros apart) a taste for monarchy?
'Pope of surrealism' is unfair, no doubt,
    And yet, it comprehends the way he chose
To issue edicts, excommunicate his friends.
    I saw his face look out from yours –
Or so it seemed – the day that I declined
    To dine in company, which led you on to say:
'Always the Englishman, you want to found
    Another church.' So, always the Englishman,
I compromised and came – Paris vaut une messe.
    For it was Paris held us on its palm,
Paris I was refusing as well as you
    And should have said no to neither:
Paris looked in on all we were to say and do,
    And every afternoon concluded with
That secular and urban miracle
    When the lights come on, not one by one,
But all at once, and the idea and actuality
    Of the place imprinted themselves on dusk,
Opening spaces undeclared by day.
    All the recurrences of that constellation
Never reunited us by that river.
    Yet, time finding us once more together
On English soil, has set us talking,
    So let me renew my unrequited question
From twenty years ago: 'Do you, Octavio,
    Work when you are walking…?'

Blaubeuren

And now the season climbs in conflagration
    Up to the summits. The thick leaves
Glow on either side of the descent
    A fire-ride carves between the trees –
A blue, unsoundable abyss. The sun
    Is pushing upwards, firing into incandescence
Lingering vapours. The tufted pinetips
    Begin to define the hilltop where a cross –
Too blatant to beckon a heart towards it –
    Stands stolid and ghostly, a dogmatic
Concrete post hardening out of mist,
    And, grey to gold, touch by touch,
The wood mass – beams breaking in –
    Visibly looms above the town. Below
Floats back a climbing bell-chime
    Out of the theological centuries: that, too,
Caught up into the burning vibrancy,
    Seems yet another surface for refraction,
Fragmenting into audible tips of flame.
    The beacon of the day – the mist has burned away now –
Blazes towards the death and resurrection
    Of the year. To be outlived by this,
By the recurrences and the generations, as today
    Has lived beyond the century of Dürer –
His rocks stand jutting from the foliage here –
    Is to say: I have lived
Between the red blaze and the white,
    I have taken the sacrament of the leaf
That spells my death, and I have asked to be,
    Breathing it in at every pore of sense,
Servant to all I see riding this wave
    Of fire and air – the circling hawk,
The leaves… no, they are butterflies
    That love the ash like leaves and then
Come dancing down from it, all lightness
    And away. Lord, make us light enough
To bear the message of this fine flame
    Rising off rooted things, and render it

Back to the earth beneath them, turning earth
    Itself, while the light still holds,
To a steady burning, a clarity
    Bordering the blue, deep fold of shadow:
Cars, weaving the woodslope road,
    Glitter like needles through the layered leaves.

The Door in the Wall

i.m. Jorge Guillén

Under the door in the wall
the slit of sun
pours out at the threshold
such an illumination,

one begins to picture
the garden in there,
making the wrinkled step
seem shadowy, bare;

but within the shadows
an underfoot world puts forth
in points of light
its facets of worth –

surfaces of such depth
you have only to eye them,
to find you are travelling
a constellation by them;

and the sun that whitens
every lightward plane
leaks up the stone jamb,
reappears again

where the flickering tangle
of thick leaves covers
the top of the wall and
ivy piles over.

So the garden in there
cannot mean merely
an ornamental perfection
when the gardener lets be

this climbing parasite
within whose folds
birds find a shelter
against rain and cold.

But let be the garden, too,
as you tread and travel
this broken pathway
where the sun does not dazzle

but claims company with
all these half-hidden things
and raising their gaze
does not ask of them wings –

fissures and grained dirt,
shucked shells and pebble,
a sprinkle of shatterings,
a grist of gravel

where the print and seal
the travelling foot has set
declares, Jorge Guillén,
the integrity of the planet.

Geese Going South

Planing in, on the autumn gusts,
   Fleeing the inclement north, they sound
More like a hunting pack, hound
   Answering hound, than fugitives from the cold:
Flocks, skeining the air-lanes
   In stately buoyancy even seem
To dance, but one's weightless dream
   Of what they feel or are, must yield
The nearer they approach. I sense the weariness
   Of wings that bring them circling down
Onto this cut corn-field
   That offers small sustenance but rest
Among its husks and straw. Rest –
   Yet they continue calling from extended throats
As they did in flight, expending still
   Energies that they will not stint
Crying to one another – is it? – encouragement.
   I break cover for a clearer sight, but they
Instantly perceive this senseless foray
   No hunter would attempt: a thousand birds
At the snap and spread of a great fan,
   A winnowing of wings, rise up
Yelping in unison, weariness turned to power,
   And tower away to a further field
Where others are arriving. I leave them there
   On the high ridge snow will soon possess.
A moon that was rising as the birds came down
   Watches me through the trees. I too descend
Towards the firefly town lights of the valley.

What does a goose, I ask myself,
Dream of among its kind, or are they all
    Of a single mind where moonlight shows
The flight-lanes they still strain towards
    Even in sleep? ... In sleep
The town beside these transient neighbours
    Scarcely dreams of their nocturnal presence
Awaiting dawn, the serpentine stirrings
    And restless moon-glossed wings,
Numb at arrival, aching to be gone.

Hamilton, USA

Picking Mushrooms by Moonlight

Strange how these tiny moons across the meadows,
Wax with the moon itself out of the shadows.
Harvest is over, yet this scattered crop,
Solidifying moonlight, drop by drop,
Answers to the urging of that O,
And so do we, exclaiming as we go,
With rounded lips translating shape to sound,
At finding so much treasure on the ground
Marked out by light. We stoop and gather there
These lunar fruits of the advancing year:
So late in time, yet timely at this date,
They show what forces linger and outwait
Each change of season, rhyme made visible
And felt on the fingertips at every pull.

Down from Colonnata

A mist keeps pushing between the peaks
    Of the serrated mountains, like the dust
Off marble from the workings underneath:
    Down from Colonnata you can hear
The quarrymen calling through the caves
    Above the reverberation of their gear
Eating through limestone. We are moving
    And so is the sun: at each angle
Of the descending road, the low light
    Meeting our eyes, surprises them whenever
It reappears striking a more vivid white
    From the crests behind us. Down
And on: the distance flashes up at us
    The flowing mercury of the sea below
That we, passing Carrara, lose
    Until it shows once more backing the plain.
But the sun has outdistanced us already,
    And reaching the level water, dipped
Beneath it, leaving a spread sheen
    Under the final height dividing us,
And across the liquid radiance there,
    A palpitation of even, marble light.

Jubilación

a letter to Juan Malpartida

You ask me what I'm doing, now I'm free –
Books, music and our garden occupy me.
All these pursuits I share (with whom you know)
For Eden always was a place for two.
But nothing is more boring than to hear
Of someone's paradise when you're not there.
Let me assure you, robbers, rain and rot
Are of a trinity that haunt this spot
So far from town, so close to naked nature,
Both vegetable and the human creature.
Having said that, now let me give a sample
Of how we make short northern days more ample.
We rise at dawn, breakfast, then walk a mile,
Greeting the early poachers with a smile
(For what is poetry itself but poaching –
Lying in wait to see what game will spring?).
Once back, we turn to music and we play
The two-piano version of some ballet,
Sacre du Printemps or Debussy's *Faune*,
On what we used to call the gramophone,
To keep the active blood still briskly moving
Until we go from dancing to improving
The muscles of the mind – 'in different voices'
Reading a stretch of Proust, a tale of Joyce's.
And so to verse. Today, the game lies low,
And Brenda, passing, pauses at the window,
Raps on the pane, beckons me outside. She
Thinks, though we can't plant yet, we still can tidy,
Clear the detritus from the frosty ground
With freezing fingers, and construct a mound
Of weeds and wood, then coax it to a red
And roaring blaze – potash for each bed,
As Virgil of *The Georgics* might have said.
I signal back my depth of inspiration,
The piece I'm finishing for *Poetry Nation*
(What nation, as a nation, ever cared

A bad peseta or a dry goose turd
For poetry?). Our Shelley's right, of course,
You can't spur on a spavined Pegasus
Or, as he puts it, 'There's no man can say
I must, I will, I shall write poetry.' –
Or he can say it and no verse appear.
As you now see (or would if you were here)
The winter sunlight sends its invitation
To shelve these mysteries of inspiration
And breathe the air – daybreak at noon, it seems,
The swift de-misting of these British beams
(Our watercolour school was full of such
Transient effects – we took them from the Dutch).
Strange how this wooded valley, like a book
Open beneath the light, repays your look
With sentences, whole passages and pages
Where space, not words, 's the medium that assuages
The thirsty eye, syntactically solid,
Unlike the smog-smudged acres of Madrid
Boiling in sun and oil. You must excuse
These loose effusions of the patriot muse.
Not everybody's smitten with this spot –
When Chatwin lived here, he declared he was not,
His cool, blue eye alighting only on
Far distant vistas Patagonian,
Untrammelled in the ties of local life,
Lost to the county, to both friends and wife.
We'd walk together, talking distant parts –
He thought we all were nomads in our hearts.
Perhaps we are, but I prefer to go
And to return, a company of two.
Hence jubilation at my *jubilación*
That we, together, leave behind our *nación*
And visit yours – or, just look up, you'll see
The vapour trails above us, westerly
The high direction of their subtle line,
Spun between Severn and Hudson, and a sign
That we shall soon be passing at that height
And, if the weather's clear, catch our last sight
Of Gloucestershire beneath us as we go.

But I must use 'la pelle et le râteau'
(Things that were images for Baudelaire),
And with the backache, spade and rake, prepare
The soil to plant our crops in on returning.
So I must pause from versing and start burning,
To anticipate the time we're once more here
In the great cycle of the ceaseless year.

Jubilación: the Spanish for 'retirement'.

The Shadow

The sun flung out at the foot of the tree
A perfect shadow on snow: we found that we
Were suddenly walking through this replica,
The arteries of this map of winter
Offering a hundred pathways up the hill
Too intricate to follow. We stood still
Among the complications of summit branches
Of a mid-field tree far from all other trees.
Or was it roots were opening through the white
An underworld thoroughfare towards daylight?
There stretched the silence of that dark frontier,
Ignoring the stir of the branches where
A wind was disturbing their quiet and
Rippled the floating shadow without sound
Like a current from beneath, as we strode through
And on into a world of untrodden snow,
The shadow all at once gone out as the sun withdrew.

Walks

The walks of our age
are like the walks of our youth:
we turned then page on page
of a legible half-truth

where what was written
was trees, contours, pathways –
and what arose as we read them
half conversation, half praise –

and the canals, walls, fields
outside of the town
extended geographies
that were and were not our own

to the foot of the rocks
whose naked strata threw
their stone gaze down at us –
a look that we could not look through.

That gaze is on us now:
a more relenting scene
returns our words to us,
tells us that what we mean

cannot contain
half the dazzle and height
surrounding us here:
words put to flight,

the silence outweighs them
yet still leans to this page
to overhear what we talk of
in the walks of our age.

The Vineyard Above the Sea

This frontal hill falls sheer to water,
  Rugged forehead whose rhythmic folds
Are of stone, not flesh – walls
  That hold up the soil and the vines between,
Whose final fruit, essence and asperity,
  Is wine like daylight, tasting of the sea.
I lift a glass of it towards the sun
  Catching, within, the forms essentialized
Of these cliff-edge vine-rows –
  Cables hoisting a harvest to the summit –
And beyond the ripple of rock-shoulders
  Bearing the load of grapes and stone,
The town itself – almost a woman's name –
  Corniglia, as tight-gripped to its headland
As to their heights these walls, floating
  Along the contours like the recollection
Of a subsided ocean that has left behind
  The print of waves. Windows, doors
In the heaped façades cast a maternal glance
  Over a geology festooned, transformed,
Where through the centuries it hunched a way
  Towards these cube-crystals of the houses,
This saline precipice, this glass of light.

Drawing Down the Moon

I place on the sill a saucer
that I fill with water:
it rocks with a tidal motion,
as if that porcelain round
contained a small sea:
this threshold ocean
throws into confusion
the image that it seizes
out of the sky – the moon
just risen, and now in pieces
beneath the window: the glass
takes in the image at its source,
a clear shard of newness,
and lets it into the house
from pane to pane
riding slowly past:
when I look again
towards the sill, its dish
of moonlight is recomposing:
it lies still, from side to side
of the ceramic circle
curving across the water,
a sleeping bride:
for the moon's sake
do not wake her,
do not shake the saucer.

The First Death

in memoriam Bruce Chatwin

The hand that reached out from a painted sleeve
    When you sensed that you were dying, gathered you
Into the picture: clothes, furs, pearls,
    Bronze of a vessel, silver of a dish
From which the grapes were overflowing. Tangible
    The minute whiteness of those pearls, the galaxies
They strung; the velvets, sleeves, the welcome
    Among convivial company; the offered hand,
All those glistening appearances that now
    Were to declare the secret of their surfaces –
Surfaces deep as roots. You told
    How you were led at that first death
Through the Venetian plenitude of a room
    Across which a glance confirmed the presence there
Of windows spilling light on this festivity,
    And running beyond them, a silhouette –
The columns of a balustrade – then sky.
    You were let into the anteroom of your heaven
By the eye, moving and attending, finding good
    Those textures it had grazed on like a food.
The second time you died without remission,
    Leaving no report on the lie of the land
Beyond that parapet's stone sill, beyond the gloss
    On all surfaces, rich and indecipherable.

In Memoriam Ángel Crespo
(1926–1995)

All things engender shadow –
the rose, the rose-arch and the meadow
sombre among surrounding trees
newly in leaf: shadow
is a continual flow
in the soliloquy we weave
within ourselves, and this
makes the diamond of the day
unreal when it insists
on permanence: but then it takes
a slow and spreading shade
from the contrasting undertone that makes
each facet seem
to both gleam and darken,
changing like the surface of a stream
whose points of light
advancing, dance
on the ripple
pulling them forward
over sunless depth. Listen
and you can hear
at the root of notes
a darker music giving form
to a music already there
filling the innocent ear
with only half its story.

By Night

Lights from the hillside farm by night
    Open three doors of fire
Across the swollen stream. It is travelling
    Freighted with the weight a season's rain
Unburdens down all the waterways
    That drain this valley. Those doors
Might well be the entrance to some mine:
    How would you lift its liquid gold,
How would you hold time that is travelling, too,
    In every gleam the light is wakening
Over the waters' face, asleep and flowing
    With its dream of flight towards what end
The winter's night awaits it with? Those strips
    Of flame, vibrant with the current bearing them,
Inscribe our sign and presence here
    Who watch these waters jostling to their fate
In the far-off, sharp sea air –
    Air of origin and end: on the gathered spate
Rides a signature of fire holding its own.

Skywriting

Three jets are streaking west:
    Trails are beginning to fray already:
The third, the last set out,
    Climbs parallel a March sky
Paying out a ruled white line:
    Skywriting like an incision,
Such surgical precision defines
    The mile between it and the others
Who have disappeared leaving behind
    Only their now ghostly tracks
That still hold to the height and map
    Their direction with a failing clarity:
The sky is higher for their passing
    Where the third plane scans its breadth.
The mere bare blue would never have shown
    That vaultlike curvature overhead,
Already evading the mathematics of the spot,
    As it blooms back, a cool canopy,
A celestial meadow, needing no measure
    But a reconnaissant eye, an ear
Aware suddenly that as they passed
    No sound accompanied arrival or vanishing
So high were their flight paths on a sky
    That has gone on expunging them since,
Leaving a clean page there for chance
    To spread wide its unravelling hieroglyphs.

Death of a Poet

i.m. Ted Hughes

It was a death that brought us south,
    Along a roadway that did not exist
When the friendship was beginning death has ended.
    How lightly, now, death leans
Above the counties and the goings-on
    Of loud arterial England. I see
A man emerge out of a tent,
    Pitched at a field's edge, his back
Towards the traffic, taking in
    The flat expanse of Sedgemoor, as if history
Had not occurred, the drumming tyres
    Creating one wide silence.
Oaks stand beside their early shadows.
    Sun makes of a man's two shadow-legs
Long blades for scissoring the way
    Across yet one more meadow, shortening it.
Hardy's rivers – Parrett, Yeo, Tone –
    Flash flood waters at us. Then,
As the flatlands cede to patchwork Devon,
    Again you cannot quite foretell the way
Dartmoor will rise up behind its mists,
    As solid as they are shifting. Sun,
Without warning, sets alight the fields,
    In anticipation of that other unison
As fire enters body, body fire,
    And every lineament gone, dissolves
The seal and simplification of human limits.
    Mourners drift out of the church,
Stand watching the slow cortège
    Of car and hearse wind through the street
To that last unmaking. The net of lanes
    Entangles our departure, hedges
Zapped spruce against the expectation
    Of another spring. Scarcely time
To recall the lanes we walked in or the coast
    That heard our midland and his northern voice

Against a wind that snatched their sounds.
   The small hawks caught the light
Below us, crossing the Hartland bays
   Over endless metamorphoses of water.
Voice-prints, like foot-prints, disappear
   But sooner; though more lingeringly
They go on fading in the ear.
   We join the highway that is England now.
The moon, a thin bronze mirror
   Reflecting nothing, a rush of cloud
Suddenly effaces. The line of oaks
   That at morning stood beside their shadows
Are shades themselves on our return.

Cotswold Journey

2001

A day before the war and driving east,
   We catch the rasp of ignited engines –
Planes practising combat above this shire
   Of Norman masonry, limestone walls.
In their quiet, they seemed so permanent
   Under the changing light. But the tower
We stand beneath is hacked by sound
   Out of the centuries it has inhabited
With such certainty. After the flash
   We stand once more on stable ground
Under chevroned arches, climb the stair
   Up to the dovecot where the priest
Once fetched the victims down that he would eat.
   The form remains, the victims have all gone
From nesting places squared in stone,
   Boxes of empty darkness now. The planes streak on
Returning out of the unsteady brightness,
   The blue that rain could smear away
But does not. Sun turns into silhouettes

The gargoyles clinging to sheer surfaces
That rise above us. Sun travels beside us
    As we penetrate deeper in, lose track
Of the plane-ways that leave no vapour trails
    To decorate their passage through
In abstract fury. Courteous walls
    Rise out of stone-crowned summits,
Prelude and then surround a dwelling space
    With church and inn – for us the solace
Of a now twilit afternoon. We explore
    Before we eat, the inn-yard and the street beyond,
Where Saxon masons, raising arch and jamb,
    Cut leaves of acanthus whose weathered surfaces
Hold onto fragile form. The night
    Slowly extinguishes their edges but bequeaths
To the mind the lasting glimmer still
    Of stone come to life. The inn
Recalls us through the village street
    And I remember how a friend once said,
Speaking with a Yorkshireman's conciseness,
    'A native gift for townscape, a parochialism
But of a Tuscan kind.' Our return
    Is silent although we travel by
Lanes tracing the outlines of the airbase
    And, there, all we manage to decipher
Is the gleam of wired restriction, barbs
    That bar us out from sterile acres
Awaiting the future in a moonless quiet.
    Rain, with the clink of the lifted latch
On our arrival, bursts from the darkness where
    East and west, preparing to unseam
The sleeping world below that height,
    Downpour drops its curtain on the past
And the cry of the muezzin infiltrates first light.

If Bach Had Been a Beekeeper

for Arvo Pärt

If Bach had been a beekeeper
he would have heard
all those notes
suspended above one another
in the air of his ear
as the differentiated swarm returning
to the exact hive
and place in the hive,
topping up the cells
with the honey of C major,
food for the listening generations,
key to their comfort
and solace of their distress
as they return and return
to those counterpointed levels
of hovering wings where
movement is dance
and the air itself
a scented garden

Above the City

It would be good
to pass the afternoon
under this lucid sky,
strolling at rooftop level
this city above the city,
all the tubular protruberances,
chimneys, triangular skylights,
sheds that have lost their gardens
spread before one. The details
are not delicate up here
among the pipes and stacks,
the solid immovables, and yet
each outcrop affords
a fresh vista
to the *promeneur solitaire* –
though only the pigeons
are properly equipped
to go on undeterred
by changes of level where
one of their flat-footed
number suddenly launches itself
off the cornice sideways
taking its shadow with it
and bursts into dowdy flower,
blossoms in feathery mid-air to become
all that we shall never be,
condemned to sit
watching from windows
the life of those airy acres
we shall never inherit.

New York

Bread and Stone

The fragment of a loaf, rejected, stale:
As beautiful as any stone, it bears
Seams, scars, a dust of flour and like a stone
If it could unfold its history,
Would speak of its time in darkness and of light
Drawing it towards the thing it is,
Hard to the hand, an obstacle to sight,
Out of an untold matrix. If a son
Ask bread of you, would stone be your reply?
Let the differentiating eye
Rest on this, and for the moment read
The seed of nourishment in it as the sun
Reveals this broken bread as textured stone,
Served out as a double feast for us
On the cloth of the commonplace miraculous.

A Rose from Fronteira

Head of a rose:
above the vase
a gaze widening –
hardly a face, and yet
the warmth has brought it forth
out of itself,
with all its folds, flakes, layers
gathered towards the world
beyond the window,
as bright as features,
as directed as a look:
rose, reader
of the book
of light.

The Holy Man

In at the gate
A tramp comes sidling up:
'I called before,' – it's now eight –
'But you were still sleeping.' He smiles
Like an actor who is perfectly sure
His audience will approve of him, offers
To tell us his story in exchange
For provision (the word is his) and lists
Tea, milk, candles and ointment:
'I have been bitten by mosquitoes –
I bless them. They give only a love bite.
Did you see the moon last night? –
I blessed that too. Did you see its halo?'
I see the love bites on his wrists.
Beard, missing teeth, chapped hands.
'The Lord told me four years ago
To take up a wandering life. I made a vow
Of celibacy then, and I have broken it
Only once. That was in Limerick.
Now I am headed from Devon to the Hebrides.
The voice of the Lord is a strange sound
Both inside and out. I shall only know
When I arrive where it is he wishes me to go.'
He pauses, provision slung across one shoulder:
'I've blessed the stream that crosses your garden' –
With this elate sidelong affirmation,
Departing he leaves behind him an unshut gate.

Eden

There was no Eden
in the beginning:

the great beasts
taller than trees
stalked their prey through glades
where the pathos of distance
had no share in the life of vegetation:

there was no eye
to catch the rain-hung grass,
the elation of sky
or earth's incalculable invitation:

and when it came, that garden,
who was it raised the wall
enclosing it in the promise
of a place not to be lost,
guarded by winged sentries
taller than trees,
of an apple not to be eaten
and the cost if it were?

It was man
made Eden.

Epilogue

The Door

Too little
has been said
of the door, its one
face turned to the night's
downpour and its other
to the shift and glisten of firelight.

Air, clasped
by this cover
into the room's book,
is filled by the turning
pages of dark and fire
as the wind shoulders the panels, or unsteadies that burning.

Not only
the storm's
breakwater, but the sudden
frontier to our concurrences, appearances,
and as full of the offer of space
as the view through a cromlech is.

For doors
are both frame and monument
to our spent time,
and too little
has been said
of our coming through and leaving by them.

from *American Scenes and Other Poems* (1966)

Afterword

David Morley

Charles Tomlinson was born on 8 January 1927 at his family home 34 Penkhull New Road, Stoke-on-Trent, the only child of Alfred and May Tomlinson. In 1930 the family moved to Gladstone Street in Etruria Vale, at the heart of The Potteries. It was for the young poet: 'a land / Too handled to be primary – all the same, / The first in feeling'. He found it full of unsuspected possibilities: the shining surfaces of flooded marl pits, furnace-light reflected on canals, Van Gogh's *Sunflowers* in a dentist's waiting room.

Stoke itself was heavily polluted. The house had for its view 'the biggest gasometer in England'. Tomlinson's mother and father took their son to a farm in Great Haywood where they would fish. Walking and fishing opened his eyes to the natural world, and to the notion that patience, contemplation, and 'wishing the fish into the net' had much in common with writing poems, an image for "capturing" he shared with his later great friend Ted Hughes.

Tomlinson's health suffered as a child. Aged ten, pleurisy and rheumatic fever kept him off school for two years and in bed for nine months. During his illness, he wrote some early poems after seeing squirrels from his window. His doctor diagnosed he would have a 'tired heart' for the rest of what he expected would be a shortened life. But Tomlinson recovered and, during the war years, attended Longton High School, Staffordshire, [motto: *Renascor* 'I am born again']. Education opened up a fresh world beyond the Midlands town. As Tomlinson commented to *The Paris Review* in 1998, 'You need two good teachers in any school, which is what we had, to get through the message of civilization—the role schools are there to fulfil'. Gerhardt Kuttner, a German Jew and a refugee from Hitler, taught him German; and a Scot, Cecil Scrimgeour, taught him French. As a teenager, Tomlinson's mind was opened to Racine, Corneille, Molière, Hugo, Baudelaire, Gautier and Verlaine; and to Schiller, Heine, Kleist, Carossa, Kant, Nietzsche, Rilke, and Thomas Mann. It was a challenging but invigorating curriculum that led Tomlinson to comment later in life, 'It was that sense of belonging to Europe, which took root early in my imagination'. His fluency in German, French, Spanish, and Italian would later lead to him becoming the foremost champion of translated poetry in Britain, and an outstanding translator of poems by, among others, Attilio Bertolucci, Octavio Paz, Cesar Vallejo and Antonio Machado. The excellence of his schoolteachers informed his own virtuosity and generosity as a university teacher later at Bristol.

While a teenager, Tomlinson met the head girl from the neighbouring school at an SPCK meeting and, later, at a dance on VE night. Brenda Raybould (b. 1928) went on to read history at Bedford College, London, followed by graduate work in art history at the Warburg and Courtauld institutes where her teachers included Ernst Gombrich, and the notorious spy, Anthony Blunt. Tomlinson himself won an exhibition in 1945 to Queens' College, Cambridge, to read English and arrived 'with Rilke in his pocket'. However, compared to the rich curriculum of school, Cambridge was an intellectual disappointment and his tutor disparaged Tomlinson's passion for pan-European literature.

Disheartened, he considered leaving to pursue a freelance career writing film scripts. Brenda, with whom he was in daily written communication, persuaded him to stay until he got his degree. The poet and critic Donald Davie returned from war service in the navy and became his tutor in his final year. Davie introduced him to a range of modernist American poets, including Marianne Moore, William Carlos Williams and Wallace Stevens (his 'Thirteen Ways of Looking at a Blackbird' became talismanic to the young poet), unleashing Tomlinson's lifelong sense for the possibilities of a transatlantic poetry. Davie and Tomlinson formed a lifelong friendship (Tomlinson called Davie DAD, after the initials of his full name). Sharing their respective interests in modernist and foreign work and becoming allies in their advocacy for a more ambitious, international poetry, they taught each other.

But what Davie chiefly taught Tomlinson was how to articulate the energy of English syntax: to develop and unfold ideas over sinuous and keenly-designed verse sentences: 'to think via syntax'. In a later interview Tomlinson reflects that the power of the sustained sentence that he derived from his reading of Wordsworth, Coleridge and Cowper, came from 'playing tunes on the verbal piano, variations on grammatic possibilities'. Tomlinson never forgot his debt to Davie, dedicating the poem 'Instead of an Essay':

Teacher and friend, what you restored to me
Was love of learning; and without that gift

A cynic's bargain could have shaped my life
To end where it began, in detestation
Of the place and man that had mistaught me.

Charles Tomlinson and Brenda Raybould married on 23 October 1948 in Willesden. From this day on 'they never made a move without each other'. Charles's debt to Brenda was absolute: she shared his fidelity to art-in-life, a life that may have felt under considerable pressure given the legacy of his childhood illness. This burden, were it ever felt, never limited them: Tomlinson's teeming *oeuvre* of poetry, essays, translations, editions, paintings, collaborations, as well as his academic duties, could never have been achieved without his wife's unstinting support.

The year that they married, Charles had decided to pursue a career as an artist having experienced an epiphany - a 'conversion' he called it - while viewing Cézanne in the Fitzwilliam Museum. His fascination with painting and painters continued later in his poems, with meditations on the processes of Van Gogh and Constable. Tomlinson concentrated on painting and graphics, and began to exhibit his work in galleries in London and Cambridge, while supplementing his living as a school teacher in Camden Town.

Between 1948 and 1951, Charles confessed he 'read a lot of Augustan poetry'. In 1951 he published a small poetry collection, *Relations and Contraries,* but was unhappy about its quality. One poem survived, in which a horse-drawn milk-float 'clips by' his windows at dawn. He wrote of it many years later, '…I was approaching the sort of thing I wanted to do, where space represented possibility and where self would have to embrace that possibility somewhat self-forgetfully, putting aside the more possessive and violent claims of personality. The embrace was, all the same, a passionate one, it seemed to me…'.

The eighteenth century, and Tomlinson's reading of Ezra Pound's *The Pisan Cantos*, Wallace Stevens's *Harmonium,* and Hart Crane's *Collected Poems,* provided what he called 'a good antidote to the effects of Dylan Thomas's romanticism, for Dylan Thomas was still the voice which sounded in one's ears as one sought for a contemporary style'. He was irked by Thomas's verbal excess. Tomlinson desired precision, tonal balance, and civility of expression. American influences were beginning to define Tomlinson's poetry as well as his poetics (he called it 'a mental emigration'). Michael Schmidt observed of Tomlinson that 'Wallace Stevens was the guiding star he initially steered by'. Schmidt puts his finger on the two characteristic voices of Tomlinson that were developing in his earlier books, 'one is intellectual, meditative, feeling its way through ideas', while the other voice engages with 'landscapes and images from the natural world'.

In 1951 Tomlinson took up a post as secretary to Percy Lubbock, the critic and friend of Henry James, which took the Tomlinsons to Lerici in Italy. Five weeks into the post Tomlinson was dismissed, an episode he wrote about in 'Class': "Those midland a's / once cost me a job / ... I was secretary at the time/to the author of *The Craft of Fiction*". The Tomlinsons were, however, given a *villino* adjoining the gardener's house where Charles painted and wrote many of the poems for his collection *The Necklace* published by Fantasy Press in 1955. This appeared with an introduction by Donald Davie; the book greatly impressed the American critic Hugh Kenner and poet Marianne Moore. Leisure time in Lerici for the young, jobless couple was spent socialising with locals, and a friendship bloomed between the Tomlinsons and the poet Paolo Bertolani. This period is vividly brought to life in his candid book of critical reflections *Some Americans* (1981). For the young Tomlinson, Liguria gave him 'so many of the elements of [his] moral vocabulary, the mysteries of light, sea, rock'. It also gave him a precise, sensuous, visual vocabulary.

Once home from Italy, Tomlinson became a lecturer in English at the University of Bristol in 1956. In1958 they bought Brook Cottage, Ozleworth Bottom, near Wotton-under-Edge. A beck, prone to flooding, ran beside the garden. One of their neighbours was Bruce Chatwin who popped by between his globe-trotting. As Tomlinson recalled, '...those famous books of his underwent much discussion beneath this very roof'.

Tomlinson's poetry circles around themes of place and return: 'Places for me', he said, 'have often been happy chances like rhyme'. Brook Cottage was the centre from which Tomlinson and his growing family flew on frequent international quests to meet and collaborate with fellow poets and artists throughout Europe, Mexico, Japan, Canada, and America. From the early 1960s to the turn of the century he was poetry's Odysseus; and many of his poems are dedicated to the poets and artists with whom he made friends.

His American adventure began with the publication of *Seeing is Believing*. A sense for passionate intelligence and clear-eyed perception informs the book, qualities he had assimilated from his European and American reading, and which were crucial to his unfurling, fastidious style of writing. The manuscript had been rejected by British publishers but, thanks to advocacy of the critic Hugh Kenner, the book appeared in New York in 1958. The event led to correspondence between Tomlinson and William Carlos Williams. In 1959 Tomlinson won an International Travelling Fellowship to visit the United States. Charles, Brenda, and their baby daughter Justine, embarked on a six month expedition, travelling by greyhound bus, writing, exploring, and befriending William Carlos Williams, Yvor Winters, and Marianne Moore. Their welcome eased the literary isolation he had felt among the English poets of The Movement, whose tapered engagement with the world frustrated him.

Tomlinson's reputation in Britain grew more secure with the publication by Oxford University Press of *Seeing is Believing* in 1960. His next collection *A Peopled Landscape* (1963) is inhabited, placed, and peopled with remembered and real characters – farmers, stone-masons, factory workers. Tomlinson and his family travelled again to America in 1962-3 where he was a visiting professor at the University of New Mexico, meeting Georgia O'Keefe, Robert Duncan, Robert Creeley, and also the 'Objectivists' Louis Zukofsky and George Oppen (whose fine-chamfered verse Tomlinson likened to carpentry). Road trips in Mexico and Arizona, as well the sense of Ozleworth as omphalos, inform *American Scenes and Other Poems* (1966). In 1967, Charles met Ezra Pound in Italy at the Spoleto Festival and began his long friendship with Octavio Paz. This dynamic period was recounted, often with a delightful lightness of touch, in *American Scenes and Other Poems* (1966).

Appearing in 1969, *The Way of a World* was a daring collection, containing an array of forms including prose poetry. It opens, as does this selection, with a *tour-de-force*: 'Swimming Chenango Lake', one of Tomlinson's most scintillating poems. No less energised are the political poems 'Prometheus', about the Russian revolution, and 'Assassin', about the death of Trotsky. Tomlinson injected a muscular diction, even *duende,* into his lucid, supple, syncopated lines and rhymes that punctuated 'the forward progress of an energetic syntax'. The jump-cut, filmic progression of 'Assassin' owed a debt to Tomlinson's early attempts at film-making. *The Way of a World* also carried pieces of lucent *ars poetica*: on the psychical and physical reality of place in 'Eden'; of the graces of moderation in 'Against Extremity'; and of the choices and happy accidents of 'The Chances of Rhyme'. Chance and choice played a role in the rediscovery of his talents as a graphic artist in 1970 as he began working in decalcomania, a technique which involves pressing paint between sheets of paper to make fortuitous imagery, and then deciding how to splice, meld, and present a final image.

Written on Water (1972) and *The Way In and Other Poems* (1974) introduced powerful autobiographical elements to Tomlinson's writing concerning the universality of place, and an unflinching exploration in 'The Marl Pits' on the origins of his poetry:

> It was a language of water, light and air
> I sought – to speak myself free of a world
> Whose stoic lethargy seemed the one reply
> To horizons and to streets that blocked them back...

While *The Way In* had its roots in Stoke, and the memory of childhood, the personal epiphanies in *The Shaft* (1978) explored Tomlinson's experiences of Venice, the Euganean Hills, Tintern Abbey, New York, and an imagined and actual Arden: '...not Eden, but Eden's rhyme...'. This Eden/Arden, as a twinned ideal and place, bedded itself in his imagination over his later collections. Tomlinson also returned with renewed power to politics and personalities in the French revolution, in the dramatic poems 'Charlotte Corday', 'Marat Dead', and 'For Danton'.

Confident, playful and unalienated collections marked his publications in the 1980s. *The Flood* (1981) recounts the dramatic, but perceptually beguiling, flooding of Brook Cottage. *Notes from New York* (1984) is a book of travel, place and playfulness, and of homely exile in poems influenced in part by his admiration for Elizabeth Bishop. *The Return* (1987) flows back to the place where his earliest poetry was written, with an elegy for his friend Paolo Bertolani. Tomlinson's subsequent collections take in continents, companionship, and the sometimes bittersweet associations that arise when memory meets reality (he mourned the changes to place wrought by tourism and environmental destruction). The Mediterranean and Gloucestershire provide subject, light, and story, for *Annunciations* (1989) and *The Door in the Wall* (1992). Retirement from academic duties made for genial, celebratory, witty poetry in *Jubilation* (1995).

In 1997 a routine cataract operation robbed Tomlinson of sight in his left eye, a loss that was a torment to one whose painterly vision was at the heart of his being as well as his writing. Tomlinson suffered depression. Brenda cheered him along by reading aloud, including the entirety of Jane Austen and *War and Peace*. In his seventy-second year, Tomlinson wrote, 'I have never felt so full of possibility. The promise of the future never felt so fecund...I think I've come through'. A late phase of his writing produced elegant, keenly-observed poetry about the landscapes and inscapes of Italy, Portugal, Greece and Spain in *The Vineyard above the Sea* (1999), *Skywriting* (2003), and *Cracks in the Universe* (2006). A *New Collected Poems*, scrupulously assembled and checked by Brenda, was published in 2009.

In addition to his poetry, Tomlinson was the editor of *The Oxford Book of Verse in English Translation* (1980), and of critical essays on Marianne Moore and William Carlos Williams, and from Spanish and Italian the work of many poets, including Attilio Bertolucci and Octavio Paz. His prose includes *Some Americans* (1981), *Poetry and Metamorphosis* (1983), *American Essays: Making it New* (2001) and *Metamorphoses: Poetry and Translation* (2003).

Tomlinson's poems won international recognition and received many prizes in Europe and the United States, including the Bennett award from the *Hudson Review* in 1993; the Flaiano poetry prize in 2001; the *New Criterion* poetry prize in 2002; and the premio internazionale di poesia Attilio Bertolucci in 2004. He was made a fellow of the Royal Society of Literature in 1974, and an honorary fellow of Queens' College, Cambridge (1974), Royal Holloway and Bedford New College, London (1991), the American Academy of Arts and Sciences (1998), and the Modern Language Association (2003). He was made a CBE in 2001 and received five honorary doctorates, including one from Bristol in 2004, and a Cholmondeley award from the Society of Authors in 1979. His academic honours included visiting professorships or fellowships at the University of New Mexico (1962-3), Colgate University, New York (1967-8 and 1989), Princeton University (1981), Union College, New York (1987), McMaster University, Ontario (1987), and the University of Keele (1989).

Charles Tomlinson's poetry occupies a prominent place in any discussion of the history of twentieth-century poetry. His reputation as a true (perhaps the only true) transatlantic poet won him acclaim from readers and critics alike, perhaps even more so in

America and continental Europe than the UK itself. After a long period of ill-health and tormenting total blindness, he died peacefully at Brook Cottage on 22 August 2015 with his family around him. He is survived by his wife Brenda and their two daughters, Justine and Juliet. The service before Charles's funeral concluded with a recording of Charles reading 'The Door', the poem that serves as epilogue to this *Selected Poems*.

★

For my part, Charles was the poetic father who invited me into his English Literature tutorials at Bristol University while I was reading for a Zoology degree. He read my poems, making precise and helpful comments. He gave me challenging reading lists to broaden my repertoire of thought, feeling, and form. His mentorship became friendship. During the opera season, Brenda, Charles and I sometimes found ourselves occupying the high seats – 'The Gods' - at The Hippodrome, and would discuss music at length. Charles's love and extraordinary knowledge of music was astonishing. As Brenda has commented, 'You only had to play two notes of a piece and he would recognise it. This was *very* important for his quite subtle sense of rhythm in his poetry'.

For many readers, this will be the first time they have read Charles Tomlinson's poetry. After Charles's funeral I was convinced that a strong selection of his poems could appeal to a new generation of readers. I sought the advice of Brenda and began the adventure of re-reading and selecting Charles's work. I also listened to the recordings of his poetry made by Richard Swigg at Keele University. Hearing Charles's poems as spoken word is to tune into their meticulous music, the 'quite subtle sense of rhythm' as Brenda puts it. Every time I listened to his poems it felt like the first time I had heard them. Every time I read his poems I wanted to share them with as many people as possible. I recommend that, as you read these poems on the page, you also speak them aloud: 'Hear with the eyes as you catch the current of their sounds'.

Personal quotations are from conversations and correspondence with Brenda Tomlinson